ACCESS SUPER CONSCIOUSNESS

About the Author

RJ Spina healed himself of permanent chest-down paralysis, severe chronic illness, and life-threatening conditions through his own authentic transcendence. He has dedicated his life to the freeing and healing of humanity on all levels. RJ is the founder and president of the nonprofit Human Advancement Through Higher Consciousness and the author of the bestselling book *Supercharged Self-Healing*. He counsels people worldwide, and his revolutionary self-healing and self-realization techniques have changed and saved the lives of many across the globe. Visit him at AscendTheFrequencies.com.

Other Books by RJ Spina

Supercharged Self-Healing

Change Your Mind

Access Super Consciousness: Raise Your Frequency to Overcome Your Biggest Obstacles

First Edition
First Printing, 2024

Cover design by Shannon McKuhen

Library of Congress Cataloging-in-Publication Data (Pending)
ISBN: 978-0-7387-7713-9

Llewellyn Publications
A Division of Llewellyn Worldwide Ltd.
2143 Wooddale Drive
Woodbury, MN 55125-2989
www.llewellyn.com

Printed in the United States of America

ACCESS SUPER CONSCIOUSNESS

Raise Your Frequency to Overcome Your Biggest Obstacles

RJ SPINA

Llewellyn Worldwide · Woodbury, MN

Dedication

This book is dedicated to all the brave souls who have wholeheartedly embraced the challenge of Self-mastery. May these authentic and supreme teachings liberate all from the delusion of identity, the hallucination of separation, and the illusion of suffering. With the utmost fervent desire of your soul, summon all your love, wisdom, and power into a single point of unbreakable focus—your self-mastery—and the liberation of the planet. I decree, the mighty power of the I Am is now set free. So shall it be!

Contents

Meditations and Exercises

Chapter 9

Chapter 10

Chapter 11

Chapter 12

Chapter 13

Appendix 1

Appendix 2

Disclaimer

The material in this book is not intended as a substitute for trained medical or psychological advice. Readers are advised to consult their personal healthcare professionals regarding treatment. The publisher and the author assume no liability for any injuries caused to the reader that may result from the reader's use of the content contained herein and recommend common sense when contemplating the practices described in the work.

Introduction

Imagine never getting stressed-out, angry, and defeated when someone says or does something that is highly discordant to you. Imagine always having the ability to not accept and agree to a personal reality that is highly toxic or undesirable. Imagine always having the ability to never get knocked off your feet again, even when a relationship ends, you get fired, or you suffer a loss in health or wealth.

Within our current timeline, human incarnation into the low frequencies of the physical universe is extremely challenging. Many of us experience unrelenting financial pressures, severe societal conditioning, and extreme brainwashing. We are the targeted recipients of trauma-based mind control and unrelenting fear-based negative bombardment from every possible angle, even angles and frequencies human beings are completely unaware of. Mounting bills, rising prices, less personal freedom, strained relationships, nonstop politicizing, job pressures, and tighter controls on making a living are not going to go away.

Just as the individual wave crashes and folds back into the vastness of the ocean, there eternally exists a state and level of consciousness where individuality dissolves and oneness is experienced. Self-mastery is the tangible, practical, and highest level of self-knowledge regardless of frequency, timeline, or location within the multiverse. It is a way to escape the bombardment and, therefore, the tyranny of the patterned subconscious egoic mind.

What Is Self-Mastery?

Self-mastery is the individualized totality and completeness of existence, tangibly known and at your command. Liberation and transcendence over the human condition are achieved through mind-body integration with your I Am, your eternal beingness.

Self-mastery does not remove you from the human experience. It affords you the ability to greatly minimize, if not totally transcend, its effects upon you in a very real and practical way. Self-mastery gives you the ever-present, moment-to-moment ability to always be rooted in something far greater and infinitely more powerful than just your beliefs, wants, intellect, and physical body. Self-mastery gives you direct access, utilization, and unification with the eternal, immortal, and undefeatable I Am.

Self-mastery carries you across hurricane waters with joy and lightness in your heart and a clear mind. No more perpetual exhaustion due to your human character swimming harder and harder against a current that doesn't exist.

What is possible for you when you work with the teachings of Self-mastery? The transformation and fulfillment you desire cannot be experienced with *mental understanding* of what Self-mastery is; you need to go beyond that. The purpose of integrating the higher-consciousness metaphysics of Self-mastery is to greatly increase the quality of your entire life—every facet from moment to moment now and forever in every single way.

Authentic enlightenment, or Self-realization, is full communion with your Higher Self. It's part of the journey and evolution of consciousness that can eventually bloom into true Self-mastery. It's like power-washing the dirty windshield of your screen of consciousness and the purification of your energy. It is tangibly seeing and understanding the Self and therefore, the greater reality with clarity, connectivity, calmness, communion, and courage perpetually.

Why Read This Book?

There are countless books written from an infinite number of perspectives. There is, however, only a handful that illuminate the inner metaphysical mastery of the mighty *I Am*. Only through extraordinarily rare states of Absolute-Realization can the supreme secrets ever be revealed. You, my friend, are holding just such a book.

The treasure of the infinite I Am cannot be captured through any concept, belief, identity, bodily sensation, or mental understanding. It cannot be reduced through the machinations of thought even by the greatest of intellects. The infinite treasure of the I Am shall forever escape all who seek its gold through the blindness of the mind/body complex. Why, you ask? Because the immeasurable I Am precedes and exceeds seeking itself.

Self-mastery is your destiny and birthright. It is always and already within you. These teachings and this book exist to simply remind you about yourself. I do warn you, you must be prepared for great loss: loss of limitation, identification, doubt, anxiety, fear, trepidation, suffering, and lack. There is nothing to gain because you are already the fulfillment of what you seek. There is only the recognition of your own full, complete I Am. A diamond is still a diamond even when it's covered in mud. Self-mastery is the letting go of everything that's gotten in the way—all your attachments, all your mental projections, all your emotionalizations, all your identifications, all so-called knowledge.

The teachings within this book—and all my books—are what I have been told during my conversations with God, whom I will refer to in this text as Source/God/Creator, to call the Wisdom That Transcends Knowledge. It will provide the underpinnings of a new Earth. This new Earth—of which many of you are here to usher in—will need new teachers. Consider this book your personal study guide.

More About Me

Roughly eight years ago, I was told I only had forty-eight hours to live due to severe sepsis. I was "permanently" paralyzed from the chest down and riddled with chronic disease and other life-threatening conditions. Through my own authentic Self-realization, I remembered how self-healing really works. I put my paralyzed and deathly ill body back together—just as I predicted I would in only 100 days. The teachings and metaphysics I utilized became the foundation of my first best-selling book *Supercharged Self-Healing.*

Since that time, I have helped thousands of people all across the globe heal themselves mentally, emotionally, physically, and spiritually. The metaphysical higher-consciousness protocols I teach awaken the direct connection to your own unlimited Higher Mind and frees you from deeply rooted subconscious and egoic limitations. Through these enlightened metaphysics, humanity can experience a superior quality of life and accelerate its own ascension and spiritual evolution. These lessons were included in my second best-selling book *Change Your Mind.*

This book, my third book as RJ Spina, has been eons in its conception and inception. It (and me) is part of the overall body of work that my Higher Self undertakes for its own evolution and for the evolution of consciousness itself. I would be remiss if I didn't clearly state that the eternal and timeless work of my Higher Self has always maintained a focus on one very specific endeavor: the evolution of consciousness with the greatest efficacy possible through the freeing of humanity on all levels. It is my true love, greatest joy, and eternal purpose.

To that end, I have curated various snippets from my live Self-mastery course that I taught June 30, 2022, through November 31, 2022. By including some of the interaction between myself and my students, it is my hope that this book will provide an extra element that other books cannot. Over the five months I taught the course, there were countless epiphanies, profound realizations, and incredible healing for my students. It is my fervent desire that you experience the same by reading and performing the meditations and exercises contained within this book.

How To Use This Book

It is truly *now* or never. Forget the concepts of a past and future and read this book with an open heart. Let its timeless truths dissolve your fragmented mind. You are not here to simply participate in the cyclical game of physical incarnation but rather master it while its degree of difficulty is on the highest setting. Any lesser challenge would be no challenge at all!

There is exponential room for growth in every single facet of your human experience. As you discover these supreme and simple teachings, you will simultaneously discover that these things are not only possible and achievable here and now, but they are already within you.

All these teachings are incredibly powerful and mind-bogglingly effective. That is true, in part, because all the teachings are prescriptive. Mental understanding of enlightened metaphysics does not invoke change, transformation, or liberation. Only tangible, direct experiential realization can liberate you from suffering and delusion.

The key to getting the most out of this book is to repeatedly perform the twenty-four meditations and exercises that accompany the Self-mastery and timeless truth teachings. Not only perform them with sincere devotion and dedication but embody them. Develop a daily practice where you perform one specific meditation multiple times a day for an entire week. Master it and experience its tangible truth within you. Then, and only then, move on to the next teaching and its accompanying meditation. Perform that meditation multiple times a day for that week until it, too, has been mastered. The appendixes include these techniques as well, so you can find them quickly.

Do not see these meditations as something to "get through and done." Self-mastery is not to be approached as something to check off from your to-do list. Refrain from letting your egoic mind turn it into a race or an accomplishment. Instead, with gentle tenacity, dedicate yourself to the freeing of your mind and body. Zero in on surrendering to the process, not any fixation for a result. Most importantly, never disengage from the discovery of the greater aspects of what you really are that only the authentic teachings of Self-mastery can provide.

The authentic teachings of genuine Self-mastery have once again been placed into their rightful hands: yours. It is my supreme honor, joy, love, passion, and responsibility to serve humanity with all my heart. There is one thing I require of you in return, my friend. I demand and command the frequency of your liberation to echo throughout the multiverse; its polyphonic symphony eternally reverberating, shattering the confines of ignorance and deceit once and for all.

Now do we broadcast the signal that rattles the cages throughout the Ages.

Awaken all sages! The fire of truth now rages!

Chapter 1
My Journey of Alchemical Transformation

My personal experiences as RJ have illuminated the enlightened understandings found in this book in the most profound and impactful way. There have been many moments in my life that have served as a catalyst (a reminder, a data point) along my journey of Self-realization. Each one has occurred to perfectly build upon the previous experiences. There could never have been one without the other, each supporting my expansion, liberation, and transcendence.

Looking back, it is clear to see how I placed these data points along the timeline of my life plan. These moments were meticulously engineered and strategically planned. I can see them all laid out and then strung together like so many pearls on a necklace. I am going to share just a few of these moments with you on my journey to Self-realization.

Childhood

My earliest childhood memories are of me leaving my body. My parents told me that I was a prolific sleepwalker. If you are going to do it, why not excel at it? I now understand, for me, there was a direct correlation to my consciousness exploration and my proclivity and propensity to sleepwalk.

I shared a bedroom with my older sister as a child. She would always fall asleep first. Perhaps, at the time, I unconsciously felt it was easier for me to leave my body during the solitude and silence of her slumber. The first time I recall leaving my body, I must have been three or four years old. I was relaxed and lying in bed. Suddenly, I found myself stuck to the ceiling directly over my bed and body.

My sister was fast asleep in her bed. My physical body was asleep as well and in my bed. Recognizing both her body and mine, I felt an overwhelming sense of total indifference. I had no attachment or identification whatsoever to my bodily form. I felt the impulse to explore, so I began to crawl along the ceiling of the bedroom toward the door. I continued this movement along the ceiling throughout the entire upstairs of my parents' house.

I remember the idea struck me to go explore downstairs as well, I can remember a flash of doubt regarding how I would make that happen. With that flash, my trip was over. I was right back in my physical body and back in bed. It was instantaneous. I knew immediately that doubt is the death of intention.

These trips outside of my physical body continued daily. Often, multiple times in a day. I realized it was my deep relaxation and focused intention that made it possible to leave my body. As my trips increased in frequency, they also increased in duration and distance.

I noticed that once my exploration began to expand beyond my parents' house, my prolific sleepwalking was birthed. I vividly recall sitting atop a local mountain top and conversing with an angel. The conversation, like all these types of interactions, was telepathic. This powerful archangel was fully embodied, with wings, a mighty sword, and wore a suit of impenetrable armor.

It was right after this conversation with my old friend did my explorations to significantly higher frequencies and exalted states of consciousness commence. Right on cue, my sleepwalking also went to new unchartered territories. As my essence ascended the frequencies and dimensions of the multiverse, I would commune and interact with other advanced beings I felt deeply connected to and part of.

When these events would occur, my physical body would not only rise from my bed but also walk a mile to the local park, take a trip to my school, or briefly sojourn to friends' respective houses. The further my consciousness went into the greater reality, the farther out into the physical world my sleepwalking took my earthly body.

During each trip my sentience took into these exalted realms, I would consciously repeat the mantra "I retain all information and wisdom contained within the realm." When I would return to my physical body, I was literally wiser for it. I was making myself remember who I Am and why I incarnated at this time.

My parents, of course, were terribly concerned about the sleepwalking and not privy to what was happening while I sleepwalked. It was around five years of age that I asked my mom where she goes when she sleeps. It was only at that moment did I realize that what was happening to me wasn't universal.

It was also around this age that I explained to my mom that I was here to change the world. I explained that what I know and will teach is going to free humanity. I told her how I would die, when, and that I planned everything. I also told her if I ever get sick, I will just heal myself. I even said that I was a God and that I needed to be here because I'm the only one that can do what must be done. Yup, I said all that. I never thought I would share this confession with the world but the work and the message (not me) are that vital.

The Year That Changed Me

My life, despite carrying a deep knowingness about things, was fairly normal. What stood out most was the horrible dynamic between my dad and me. I did not have the best relationship with my father. He was raised old-school Italian and went to catholic school through his high school graduation. He was very free with his hands but not so much with his love.

Within a very brief window of time during the year of 1995, I experienced a lot of loss. First, my best friend—my dog Clyde—passed away. My heart was broken. Then, my sister's husband passed away at the tender age of twenty-seven. My grandmother, who I was extremely close to and who lived downstairs in our two-family house, passed away. My grandfather from downstairs passed too. Their son, my uncle Paul, who always felt like my father, also passed. My best friend from high school passed away. All this combined with the escalating violence in my parents' house, became too much for me. By the time I turned twenty-four, I was suicidal.

I was with nearly all of those precious beings as they passed. Some of their deaths were absolutely devastating and traumatic. These moments haunted me. They tormented my every waking moment. I knew it was in me to be able to help them, to heal them, and I couldn't bring it out. It drove me insane. I loved them all so dearly. I was seething with rage, completely heart-broken, and utterly despondent. I didn't want to be here anymore. There was no point.

At this time, I met a very unusual man named Rich while out to lunch with two acquaintances. He was roughly fifteen years older than me. His eyes carried so much purity and depth that it comforted me. He told me he was a psychic and that I needed to come to a group reading he was giving on Friday. He asked me if I was open to it. I sheepishly nodded in agreement. Nobody knew I planned on killing myself Saturday.

I was the last to arrive to Rich's reading on Friday. There were ten of us total. Rich explained that he was going to go around the room, one-by-one, and let us know what he picks up from the spirit realm. As he went around the room, I could tell that he was picking up something, but my simmering anger and deep despair was like quicksand. I was being swallowed up and pulled under. I couldn't escape its grip.

I was last to get a reading. When Rich got around me, he said that Uncle Paul was standing next to me. He said he was wearing a leather cowboy hat and a suede vest. My heart stopped. I had only met Rich once at lunch. He knew nothing of me or my life. Uncle Paul always wore his leather cowboy hat and suede vest. Always.

He said Uncle Paul was always with me and that he would never let anything happen to me. Tears were beginning to well up, and it took what little resolve I had left to keep from erupting into an emotional mess.

"If that's true, if my uncle is really here, then ask him what he got for me on my fifth birthday."

Without batting an eye Rich said, "He got you that yellow Evel Knievel motorcycle you used to ride up and down in front of the house."

I lost it. I mean *lost it.* My knees buckled and I fell to the ground. I wept like I have never wept before or since. At some point after, I remember being seated on Rich's couch. Rich held a raffle for all the guests. The prize was a twelve-inch golden angel figurine. He looked right at me as he reached inside the punch bowl full of crumpled pieces of paper with our names scribbled on them. Without looking at the name on the paper, and never breaking eye contact with me, he said, "The winner is RJ. An angel for an angel." I couldn't move a muscle.

Everyone said their goodbyes and filed out. Rich sat down next to me and said nothing. I was motionless and speechless. What was about to happen would change the course of my life forever.

"RJ, I have to ask you a question."

The pregnant pause between those words and his next ones seemed to carry more import than anything I had ever experienced in my life.

"When is a rose not a rose?"

My entire body shifted. I felt electricity go right through my spine. I immediately turned to him, without thinking but with knowing and said, "When one fails to recognize one as such."

He looked deeply into my eyes and implored, "You don't understand. You... YOU are the wisest of men. You must wake up or you will never make it in this life."

"I'm the wisest of men?! I certainly don't feel like it. I don't want to be here anymore. Everyone I love is gone."

The tears returned and my despair swallowed me whole.

"Listen to me. You must meditate. You must. Your life depends upon it."

Truth is, I just wanted him to stop. I got up from the couch. I put on my denim jacket and made my way toward the front door. Rich met me there and handed me the angel. He looked at me. I could see oceans of time in his eyes.

"You must. Promise me."

I said nothing and exited his apartment. I willed myself to get through the tiny parking lot of Rich's apartment complex. Finally, I unlocked the door and sat down in the driver's seat of my red Pontiac Fiero. I placed the angel figurine in the passenger seat. This would all be over soon, I thought to myself. I turned on the ignition and silently drove home.

Destiny

I got home late. It was around 11:30 PM. My parents were asleep. My sister no longer lived in the house. I entered my downstairs bedroom and placed the angel on my desk. In the drawer just beneath it was a loaded gun. The pull to open that drawer was increasing. I needed the agony, the rage, the despair to end. I couldn't take it anymore.

I stared at the drawer for what seemed like an eternity. I knew I needed to end my life. It just didn't work out. It was all too painful and brutish. The tears of regret streamed down my cheeks. I reached for the drawer ... and then it happened.

Every pipe throughout the entire house began to ping. It was like a symphony. The furnace kicked on, my night light flickered, and my bed moved. It was so unmistakable that even in my deeply despondent state, it made me stop in my tracks.

"Uncle Paul," I said through my tears and heaving emotions. The pipes stopped, the bed became still, the furnace turned off. I knew. In that moment I knew. It was now or never.

"Fine." I said out loud. I sat at the at edge of my bed with the intention to meditate. Something powerful and ancient came over me. I was remembering. Without ever having been taught any formal meditation, I put myself into perfect meditative posture. I closed my eyes, and I was spontaneously inspired to perform a meditation that I still teach to this day. Within twenty seconds, my third eye opened fully. A screen dropped down within my consciousness. The veil of delusion was being removed. What I saw, what I experienced, changed me forever.

In about twelve seconds I understood myself, and the role I play when I incarnate, more than I had in my previous twenty-four years combined. I had awakened to my True Self. I felt a calmness, a clarity, and a resoluteness that had been dormant but no longer.

I never suffered the longings of suicide, despair, or disempowerment again. It had been lifted. This was my first awakening as an adult. I slept like a baby that night. At peace. Free. I called Rich the next morning to tell him what happened. He said, "Of course. You need to come over here. We have a lot of work to do."

One Year Later

Rich and I began working together daily. We would practice by giving past life readings to people. We would act as a checks and balances system for one another. We would time travel and learn how to project our consciousness anywhere into the multiverse on command. We would consult with deceased doctors to see if they could offer any hidden insights that we could relay to people who came to us for healing. We solved ancient mysteries that stumped humanity for eons of times.

Rich is, from my perspective, by far and without question, the best medium and trance channel on this planet. It's not even close. He is also one of the most evolved souls to ever walk this Earth.

Nobody knows him or anything about him, and he prefers to keep it that way.

Let me expand, albeit briefly, on Rich's profound abilities. In 1995, I spoke and spent quality time (well over 150 different occasions) chatting and hanging out with Eleanor Roosevelt.

Let me be clear. I wasn't channeling Eleanor or communing with her energetically. Rich is so highly skilled and pure; he would allow her to completely inhabit and take over his body. She would shuffle around Rich's apartment, go grocery shopping with me, or sit in the passenger seat and wave to other drivers! We would have tea together, watch the news together, break bread together, and talk about everything together. Being inundated within a world that is beyond our agreed-upon limitations was part of my journey of enlightenment.

Eleanor is a giant among souls and cares deeply about humanity. She is wise, compassionate, strong-willed, and has a wicked sense of humor! She loves to learn about the true mastery of the mystic arts. The only thing I will share explicitly about what Eleanor and I spoke about is regarding what she said to me about Rich.

"My dear, you are the only soul Rich trusts. You are the only soul that he feels he can count on."

"I feel the same way about him."

"I know you do, my dear. The familiarity and trust run deep."

She placed her hand upon mine and squeezed it ever-so-gently.

"Enjoy your time together. Your interaction in this lifetime will be relatively brief. Make sure it helps prepare you for what you are going to do in this life. He's not the only one counting on you, my dear."

No pressure.

The One Dollar Bill

One late but unusually warm fall afternoon in upstate New York, Rich and I were seated on a park bench observing the digital matrix we call physical reality parade go by. Moms proudly displaying their recent offspring in various baby chest-harnesses, groups of tightly packed teenagers all bobbing their heads as their headphones blare Madonna, mid-sized dogs not-so-gently steering their stumbling owners to wherever the scent is most enticing.

We both, without conferring with one another, went into meditation. Rich with his eyes closed and mine forever open. The shapes and forms of this world begin to disassemble. More of the Self and the Greater Reality become obvious and tangible. The door of my Higher Mind is thrown open. All the world's a stage and now you remember your lines. The mighty I Am knows it is running the show.

Rich spotted him first. Without breaking his meditation or opening his eyes, he very quietly said to me, "Do you see him? The lower astral. Just past the trimmed trees on the left. Right beside the broken fountain."

As soon as he said it, he came into view. He was still dressed in full uniform. As soon as I located him, he spotted me and then Rich. He immediately began to make his way to us.

"You talk to him, RJ. He needs help."

I was shocked by what I saw but not startled. It was clear none of the park residents could see him as he was outside of the third frequency. He came right up to Rich and me. He was confused, tired, and very lost.

"Where am I?"

"You're in upstate New York," I said.

"I want to get to my plantation."

"I'll help you. It's okay. Do you know who you are?"

"Of course. You are familiar to me. Did we win?"

"Yes."

"Are you sure?"

"Yes. I'll show you."

I reached into my wallet, took out a single one dollar bill, and showed it to him.

"It's you, George. You did it. We won the war."

With this visual proof, the great George Washington slowly nodded his head. I could feel his intense pride and incredible determination. It was moving. I don't think Rich could speak.

"You did an amazing job, George. We are so proud of you. We all owe you a tremendous debt of gratitude. Me especially. Listen, I know how to get you to your plantation. First, just close your eyes. See it clearly in your mind. Every single detail. Feel the bark on the trees surrounding the estate. Smell the pine. Listen to the birds chirping."

With that, George disappeared. Rich and I sat in awe and speechless on the park bench for quite a while. The comings and goings of the patrons of the park never skipped beat. None was wiser to what just transpired. Rich finally turned to me. With a wry smile curled around his face he said, "Good thing you had a dollar. I only carry large bills."

The Mothers of Destiny

"I see it clearly," I relayed to Rich. "The chair works with the higher more subtle aspects of the subconscious mind. It reads what is embedded in these layers by using a very specific pulse and wavelength of light."

As I sat on his couch, Rich, sitting in the lotus position on the floor, feverishly wrote down everything as quickly as I was relaying. It was all coming to me like a dream but in a kind of hyper-stylized reality. It was more real than our current sense of what "real" is.

"The chair—the technology—it lets you see and watch all your past lives. And anyone else's too."

It was challenging to keep my subtle concentration perfectly attuned to what I had tapped into because I was genuinely excited about the discovery.

"RJ, what year is this?"

"5496. It's the end of a specific cycle of consciousness. The chair represents humanity graduating into a new level of self-understanding. Everything and everyone here are so different. We are all at peace.

We live in harmony with everything. There is only one small patch of the earth where those who wish to war only war with themselves. It's a self-imposed prison. They want to be there. They still reject love."

I became emotional and lost the connection. I sat back on the couch and purposely slowed my heart rate down. I took a sip of water and looked at Rich. The energies in the room were extremely high. It felt like something monumental was about to happen.

Rich dropped his notebook and joined me on the couch. He sat on the opposite end, reached over to the side table, and lit three candles. We both became extraordinarily still. Our senses were incredibly heightened. He could feel it.

The flames on the candles began to flutter. The air became completely still. The temperature dropped. My heart started opening. I felt an overwhelming sense of love. Then, it happened.

Rich began to weep. I could not speak nor think. It felt like my physical body had disintegrated. She was in the room. She stood before us, more heavenly than anything in this world.

Rich began reciting the Hail Mary over and over through tears of joy.

She slowly reached out and touched my face. The electricity, the familiar love, that went through me almost lifted me off the couch. She looked deeply into my eyes. I have never felt such tenderness and love like this in my life. I wasn't breathing. There was no need.

"I am with you, my dear. The golden fibers within your heart will protect you, as I will, in this life. You will triumph. Your love and devotion for humanity has carried you here and it is God's love that will heal all."

I could not speak or move. It was like a trance, but I was completely lucid and present. I was being bathed in the pristine energy of this luminous being. Her inner beauty, her essence, healed my heart. In that very moment, she disappeared. I wasn't in the living room of Rich's apartment anymore, but my body was.

I could feel a massively powerful energy coming, almost like it was separating space and time. Something was making its way here and now. I felt so completely loved and overwhelmed that I began to weep.

Just as I closed my eyes to blink away the tears, the Great Mother of Mercy appeared right where Mary had stood. Rich, through a torrent of tears, started bowing his head over and over in complete reverence. The majestic power and God-like compassion that emanated from Kwan Yen was the most profound and momentous moment of my life.

She gently put her hand atop my head. It felt like my brain had been removed. My entire being was filled with such endless compassion and forgiveness that I thought I died. Part of me wished I did. I would have gladly returned with them, but it was clear I was being gifted something far greater than liberation. I had been blessed, reminded, and anointed by the Great Mother.

I have literally never been the same since that night. As I write this, just as they have always known, let it be known. I will never let them or humanity down. Never. Not even death can stop me.

Liberated Consciousness

I remember the very instant I woke from emergency lifesaving surgery on April 23, 2016. I looked to my left just past the stack of health monitors and medical equipment. The analog clock read 3AM precisely. I glanced down toward my feet to see if I still had my body. With my right hand, I touched my left shoulder and chest to see if I could still feel them.

Once my hand traveled down to my solar plexus, all manner of sensation was gone. From my chest down, my body was as lifeless and immovable as a dead tree buried in the sand. I could not feel or move anything from the chest down. Nothing was different, in that sense. I was paralyzed before the surgery. Everything else, on the other hand, was completely different.

The destruction of my physical body was the liberation of my consciousness. I was free. I was unbounded by anything. I had full communion and connectivity with my Higher Self and God. I had awakened once again into authentic cosmic consciousness. The remembering of the enlightened metaphysics of self-healing and Self-realization was palpable. I already knew I would heal myself.

My conscious mind had full access to the entire roadmap of how to put my destroyed, paralyzed, deathly sick, and disease-ridden body back together. I knew that I would un-paralyze and heal myself in exactly one hundred days. I knew—I always knew—that there exists nothing in this world, or any world for that matter, that could ever stop me.

This Wisdom That Transcends Knowledge was akin to a muscle memory. All the times I used to say, "If I get sick, I will just heal myself," was now a tangible reality. I always knew that I knew, but now I *know*. In that moment, it was a forgone conclusion that I would transcend the limitations of human understanding. I was ready to endure anything and everything to prove to myself, yet again, that I could put my destroyed and paralyzed body back together.

I wasn't just ready for this impossible challenge. My Higher Mind and will were so locked into a single focus that absolutely nothing could derail me. I mean *nothing*. God wants this done!

I was told, immediately and repeatedly by a well-meaning, well-educated team of experts that walking was impossible. Absolutely impossible. That I was in deep denial of being a paraplegic. That I was delusional from the anesthesia. I was informed again and again that I will never be able to stop taking all the medications and drugs because healing chronic disease doesn't work that way (self-healing).

A few weeks later, I was accompanied by hospital and rehabilitation staff during my one and only trip home while still living at the facility for the sole purpose of having my house retrofitted because I was and would always be a paraplegic. I was told, hundreds of times, that it was not possible to get better, let alone transcend my grim condition. I bit my tongue. Every. Single. Time. I never identified with a single projection that was relentlessly and perpetually placed upon me.

The one hundred days immediately following my waking up from emergency surgery were without question the most challenging, excruciatingly painful, absolutely harrowing, beyond rewarding, and destiny laden that one could ever experience. My talents and abilities kept unfurling by the second. They needed to because the challenge was that great.

There are no limitations except the ones you believe to be real and true. There are no locks and bolts to anything. Let my overcoming chest-down paralysis and disease be your permission slip to do the impossible for yourself.

Use this book to free yourself from suffering. Use my incarnation to liberate yourself from bondage once and for all. Let's get started.

Chapter 2
Separateness to Oneness

When we devote ourselves to clarity, calmness, connectivity, and communion with the Oneself within, we walk with God. My work with Self-mastery has connected me to the super-conscious and directly to the higher power, which I know as God, but we can refer to as Source/God/Creator. I speak directly to this power and that connection is how I have this knowledge and guidance to share with you.

Source/God/Creator has shared with me that we are not physical beings. We are energy beings—to be more accurate, we are sentience given a body of energy—having a temporary physical experience. Throughout this text, I will refer to our being as sentience.

Sentience is a divine intelligence. It is the I Am. It is the Source/God/Creator within us all. From a human perspective, sentience is our level of love and wisdom whose subsets are our talents and abilities. That is what we are. This sentience has been given energy to create with. This is what it means to be created in God's image.

Space-time creates the experience of separateness, which births the concept of relationships. This temporary state of delusion leads to duality. When we limit our sentience to body consciousness, an illusory and transient subject/object paradigm encases, fragments, and compartmentalizes universal super consciousness. This contraction of consciousness prevents the tangible experience of our collective Higher Mind and eternal Oneness.

Through the cessation analysis, the dualistic nature of our fragmented lower consciousness can cease to exist. As the subject/object paradigm disintegrates, so does your experience of separation from Source/God/Creator and therefore all life. Duality no longer exists. The One who sees through your eyes sees through all eyes. It's all God. See and experience yourself and everyone this way now.

Do not seek to understand through a subject/object paradigm. This construct is the collapsing of consciousness, an illusion born of the fragmented mind. Instead, know the truth. Know thyself—the Oneself within us all. Only by the eternal silencing of your finite mind will the polyphonic symphony of existence be heard and tangibly known once again.

Separateness to Oneness is how we walk with God.

MEDITATION
Experience Separateness to Oneness

Close your eyes, take a deep breath in through the nose, and exhale out the mouth. Repeat this three times.

Pretend you just arrived here. No past, no future. Imagine what it would feel like to abandon all personal agendas. Let the purity of non-desire and its supreme vibration wash over you completely. Let it forever change your immortal state of being. Know that everyone, all existence, at its core is precisely this: agenda-less and free. Now, see all life with the eyes of purity.

Journal what this experience is like.

Everything Is One

There's no more important time for these teachings than right now. When we experience higher frequencies and higher dimensions within our consciousness, we are beyond space-time.

The Oneness is tangible because without space there is no fragmented mind that conceptualizes "relationships." It's obvious that there are no others. Everything is one, therefore everything is designed for us to come together as one.

Let's look at it through the peanut-butter-cookie analogy. You make the batter, adding peanut butter, coconut shavings, chocolate, walnuts, et cetera. Then, you start placing the dollops on the cookie sheet. No matter how careful you are, each one of those new little cookie doughs are different. Some have more chocolate, some have more peanut butter, some are rounder, flatter, bigger, odd-shaped, have more coconut, et cetera. No two are the same. Each one is separate and totally unique. But a minute ago they were all one. It is the same with us.

It's space-time that gives us the temporary experience of separation—and through separation—the concept of relationships is formed. This spawns the subject/object paradigm and through subject/object paradigm, we create duality. Now, once subject/object paradigm is created and duality is experienced, we are now, from my perspective, lost. The result will be endless variations of suffering because of this delusion.

During my Self-mastery class, a student asked me, "RJ, so to walk with God, we walk with our Higher Self outside of space and time by true meditation?"

Just to be annoying, I gave two completely different and contradictory answers: Yes and no. It is possible to experience this oneness even while experiencing the confines of space and time. So that's really the key, to experience the Oneness even when all the way "down here."

We all are our Higher Mind. We are a Higher Self, one part of the totality of a Higher Mind that resides in much higher dimensions. Our Higher Self exists way outside of space-time. The Higher Self is experiencing beyond space-time and within space-time concurrently.

We want to be able to operate from that holistic state of consciousness, even while immersed within space-time. So, we have the experience of space-time. We're in the physical, but not of the physical, as Master Sananda—the being known as Christ—has said.

In the physical, but not of the physical. This is exactly what I am talking about when we speak about these things. The Higher Mind, what you really are, is like a mansion. All the frequencies and dimensions of the multiverse are within your Higher Mind. This is what Christ was talking about when he said, "There are many rooms in my father's house." He's talking about all the different frequencies, dimensions, and parallel conditions of the multiverse. Same exact thing. This is simply how I explain and teach it from a metaphysical perspective.

This world is projected through you. Seeing happens inside you, hearing happens inside you, everything happens inside you. This world is projected outwardly through you. This is how a hologram works. Everything is contained within. You cut off a little piece of a hologram and look through it, the entirety of the hologram is contained within that one little piece. This is how we truly are.

The Oneness has temporary individuality, but that individuality contains everything. Self-mastery is the accessing and the experiencing of the totality of things, even while experiencing what we would call temporary individuality.

Not of the Physical

At this point, a student interjected, saying, "It makes sense *in* the physical, but not *of* the physical."

Yes. It means don't identify yourself as a body and part of the world as physical, if that makes sense. We're not a physical being. We are sentience given a body of energy, having a physical experience. We're a fractal of Source/God/Creator that exists outside of space-time and within space-time simultaneously. There's nothing physical about us, or anything for that matter. Even a solid is empty space, it's just energy. Even scientists today will tell you that.

Our biological garment, our physical body and its incredibly limited physical sensory perceptions just don't offer the holistic perspective or bandwidth to perceive this. Therefore, it remains intangible for the lower consciousness, or human mind, but it's true, nonetheless. What is solid is empty space or temporarily patterned energy.

We're not physical beings. What we are has no name, no image, no form. So, to be in the physical, but not of the physical, as Christ said, is to be here but not of it. Do not identify with it. Keep the I Am pure and untainted. "I Am the light, and I Am the way." Feel how that statement now means so much more metaphysically. I Am means God is. Sit with these profound teachings. Let the mind become still.

When you are completely attuned to the I Am, you are attuned to Source/God/Creator because that is Source/God/Creator. You'll be able to reconnect and commune with all life. To turn separateness into Oneness is to realize the truth. The being that's looking through my eyes is the same being that's looking through all eyes. It's all Source/God/Creator.

The temporary experience of separation leads to duality. Now there's a "me" and a "you." When we limit our sentience to just body consciousness (five physical senses and the logic, and linear-bound intellect) an illusionary and transient subject/object paradigm encases, fragments, and compartmentalizes universal super consciousness. The Oneness has disappeared and is replaced with the subject/object paradigm. Duality.

This understanding should be taught everywhere, starting with our children. How different would this world be with just this understanding? Maybe, someday. If there's anyone who wants to fund an institution of enlightened higher consciousness, you know where to find me.

How to Transcend the Subject/Object Paradigm

The contraction of consciousness prevents the tangible experience of our collective Higher Mind and eternal oneness. Now for this to begin to germinate within you, to experience this tangibly, you must stop analyzing things and judging. Be present.

Through the cessation of analysis, the dualistic nature of our fragmented lower consciousness will cease to exist. As the subject/object paradigm disintegrates, there's no me judging you. When that me is gone, the subject/object paradigm disintegrates. So will your experience of separation from Source/God/Creator, and therefore all life because there's no "you" operating from a dualistic subject/object, paradigm. Duality no longer exists. Remember that it's all God. And when you see yourself in others, what harm can you do? See and experience yourself in everyone this way.

A student asked, "Master RJ, is there a shortcut for this?"

I replied, "Are you in a rush? We just got started."

The students laughed and I continued.

The seer, what is seen, and the act of seeing are all the same thing. There is your shortcut for enlightenment. Do not seek to understand through a subject/object paradigm. Nothing is understood from there. As soon as there's a subject/object paradigm, consciousness has been broken, there's no more oneness. Consciousness has collapsed into a subject/object paradigm.

Trying to analyze and figure things out from a subject/object paradigm is pointless. You'll just lead yourself astray. Look at the world. That's what happens by approaching things from a subject/object paradigm. This collapsing of consciousness is a temporary but persistent illusion born of the unawakened mind. Know the truth, know your Self—the One Self within us all.

Everyone talks about the silence of meditation. You can go way past silence. What do they call it, the music of the spheres? You want to hear angels sing, you want to hear the symphony of existence? In the beginning was the word. And that word was sound.

Follow these teachings. This is how liberation occurs. Separateness to Oneness is how we walk with Source/God/Creator. Just be yourself. Your true self. It's all that matters. Self-mastery is all that matters because you are everything. The multiverse is designed for your Self-mastery—everything is designed for you to fully realize your Self.

Frequencies and Dimensions of the Multiverse

During a session, a student asked, "Master RJ, is there duality and separateness in all the frequencies of the first dimension?" This led to a longer discussion on frequencies and dimensions of the multiverse.

The answer to the question is yes, in the first dimension. The tangible experience of it is less and less as you ascend the frequencies. I don't want to bathe us in endless facts because esoteric wisdom can be misused as fodder for the spiritual ego. The point is to tangibly experience these things through meditation, not just listen to me talk about it but for you to experience the depth of the Self. This is why these teachings are here. For you to tangibly experience them firsthand.

That being said, I will elaborate just a little. There are twelve full dimensions. We're not in the third dimension. We're in the third frequency of the first full dimension.

It has been explained and shown to me by Source/God/Creator that energy exists frequentially, not dimensionally. Dimensions house energy. The entire physical universe is the first full dimension. After the first full dimension, from a human perspective, there's no sense of physicality to anything.

Dimensions two through twelve are completely different energetic environments that provide a multitude of various states of being and states of consciousness. But there is no physicality, none whatsoever, above the first full dimension. Dimensions two through twelve are areas within the multiversal structure where the myriad of Higher Selves reside who project aspects of themselves—a soul—into the first dimension so it can experience the physical universe.

Humans and Aliens

The first full dimension contains the entire physical universe. When we hear about aliens and different beings that exist in the fourth, fifth, or sixth dimensions, they're talking about frequencies not dimensions. The Higher Selves of humans and aliens most likely reside in the third, fourth, fifth, and (rarely) the sixth full dimension.

Very few Higher Selves reside in the seventh dimension or higher. The upper frequencies of the sixth full dimension and beyond is the realm of the Ascended Masters.

In terms of different races, even humanoids, humans, and aliens can be experiencing Earth in different frequencies. Those are the fourth through the twelfth frequencies. All those environments and beings still have a physicality to them. Once you get to the twelfth frequency of the first full dimension, there's really is no physicality to anything whatsoever.

There is a thirteenth frequency, which is kind of like a viewing station. You can look at the entire physical universe and watch life, so to speak, take place. That's the thirteenth frequency.

All physicality belongs within the first full dimension. In that dimension, the bottom three frequencies band together to form one environment. We are in the third frequency, which is what gives us height, weight, and width. That's why we call it a three-dimensional reality. Because the lower frequencies are so dense energetically, they must band together to support one environment.

But, as was stated earlier, all energy exists frequentially, not dimensionally. A frequency is an assignation of energy. To be able to tangibly experience your own Higher Mind, and therefore the greater reality clearly and concisely, requires a very detached perspective along with a certain level of sentience to process and understand it.

Beyond Human Understanding

After the thirteenth frequency viewing deck, there's a continuum. It's a band between the membrane of the first full dimension that you must transcend to enter the second full dimension. Once you go into the second full dimension, there's no physicality whatsoever. None.

Space-time is no longer experienced the way that we experience space-time. Until you experience these things through astral projection, meditation, or when you're disincarnate, intellectual understanding offers no Self-knowledge or liberation. There is no freedom within the confines of the intellect. The Self is well beyond all mental understandings.

What people call fourth-dimensional beings, or fifth- and sixth-dimensional, are actually fourth-, fifth-, or sixth-frequency beings. Once you get to the seventh frequency, that state of consciousness is so expansive and so holistic that from a human perspective, you can no longer be negatively oriented and exist within the seventh frequency. The Oneness of everything is obvious and tangible.

Having disharmonious intention or doing something "negative" to someone else, you recognize you're doing it to yourself. Down here, we're still too brainwashed and conditioned for materialism. We therefore remain clueless, and woefully unawakened to realize the truth. That truth is: whatever you do to someone, you're doing to yourself. It's all Source/God/Creator. Whatever you do to someone else, you're doing to God. I mean it. It's all God.

Ascended Masters

Once you reach the seventh frequency, what people mistakenly call the seventh density or the seventh dimension, everything is exceedingly loving, positive, benevolent, and wise. I think it's also interesting that Buddha, Christ, Saint Germain, Mahavatar Babaji, Paramahansa Yogananda, El Moriya, Djwal Khul—the old-school Ascended Masters, the true timeless teachers of humanity—those higher selves who project aspects of themselves that we know as Ascended Masters, those higher selves exist from the seventh full dimension and up.

All Source/God/Creator entities (the 12 Elohim) want to experience what each other is doing. One way they do this is to project a smaller version of themselves called a Higher Self or Totality into the environment created by each other to experience, learn, and evolve and assist one another in their respective evolution.

The Elohim and their projected aspects don't just interact with incarnate civilizations, they are the architects of these advanced civilizations. They help propel them and humanity forward with the ascension process because they, along with their projected aspects or souls, are supremely high-frequency beings. This process, as it directly relates to conception and inception of what we call humanity, started billions of years ago.

Human evolution science will differ from this, but through my Higher Self interactions with Source/God/Creator, I was shown that the form that we now recognize and label as human dates back roughly eighteen million years ago. Prior, the form would not be classified as human. The Ascended Masters have played the role of teachers as far back as this time.

Each Ascended Master is associated with and born directly from a specific Elohim. Below is a list of the Ascended Masters that have incarnated on Earth and continue to this day. Typically, an Ascended Master is not recognized as one during their incarnation. It is only in hindsight after a few hundred years have passed do we get a clearer perspective on who and what they really are.

Ascended Masters are not part of the evolutionary cycle. Rather they are inserted into it, like a wild card shuffled into the deck. They are accelerants for the entire evolutionary process. We can think of Ascended Masters as finished products. They have fully realized the immeasurable I Am. They have no interest or need to accrue sentience. Rather, they are impelled and compelled to share their immense love and wisdom so others may learn and evolve from them.

Ascended Masters are free agents. They come and go as they please. They go where they are most needed and are only bound by the commitments they themselves make. They are beyond accruing karma and even the law of cause and effect. They are beings of pure cause and quite often know who and what they are. They operate in a highly detached way and their benevolence cannot be compromised.

Ascended Masters have a high-frequency bubble around them that they build. It allows them to operate with more of their normal higher intuitive functionality even while incarnate in the lower frequencies. This energetic construct has been loosely referred to as a Merkabah. You can think of this construct like a spaceship that affords the passengers an environment conducive to their normal surroundings. In the case of a Master, rather than using physical materials to build their spaceship, they construct it purely of energy.

Upon leaving their incarnation, they often do not bother with life reviews, as they simply already and consciously know what needs to be done next and make modifications as they go. Some will even request, prior to reincarnating, that their guides and helpers remain silent during the incarnation as way of increasing their level difficulty and challenge while incarnate.

Ascended Masters are the true teachers of humanity and have chosen to come here purely of service. They have played many roles here on Earth as well as within other systems of worlds. Like an exotic flower not germane to the local environment, we cannot take our eyes off them. They are often totally mesmerizing and exude a presence, authority, and power that is literally otherworldly.

Let's look at a list and synopsis of the thirteen old-school or original **Ascended Masters:**

Maitreya is an Ascended Master who has not incarnated yet. He feels the consciousness has not awakened enough to properly work with the teachings he will embody. He does work with souls who are open enough to connect with him and his level of sentience. His consciousness can be seen as the perfect blending of Hinduism, Buddhism, and metaphysics. His focus is to help humanity transcend the need to incarnate and learn how to work with the environment optimally. He will be taking over, through a series of incarnations, after Master R or Saint Germain completes his current cycle of work on earth.

Hilarion is an Ascended Master who rarely incarnates and focuses on healing through technology. He likes to work telepathically with those in med-tech and innovative sciences. He plants revolutionary ideas in the minds of those who are open and receptive to true inspiration and benevolence through innovation and technology.

Confucius is an Ascended Master who is drawn to the profundity of transcendent philosophy through mental acuity. He has a deep understanding of the mind and how it works. He has mastered the purification of thought processes and how to align One Self with proper actions and behaviors. He teachings help us stay on track with our life plan. Not driven to make tangible his sentience through human doingness, he never bothered to capture his wisdom through writings. Those learning directly from him did and thankfully so.

El Morya is part of our God. He is an extremely dedicated servant who works tirelessly for humanity. Some of his incarnations include High Priest of Atlantis, a Tibetan Master, Abraham, one of the Three Wisemen, King Arthur, Thomas Becket, and Sri Yukteswar, just to name a few. His female incarnations are known as **Lady Master Lotus.** Those incarnations include Elizabeth 1, Joan of Arc, and most recently Edna Ballard, who channeled Saint Germain with the I Am Discourses during the early twentieth century. She left her body February 11, 1971. Both El Morya and Lady Master Lotus do a lot of work with Saint Germain.

Jesus is a single incarnation of an Ascended Master known as **Master Sananda.** Other incarnations include Enoch, Adam, and High Priest of Atlantis and several off-world incarnations. Jesus mastered purification on every level, which is where we derived the term *Christ.* He embodied how to be in the physical but not of the physical. He taught humanity how to change their thoughts, actions, and behaviors to be more loving and purer. His incarnation and his teachings changed the frequency of humanity and the planet forever. This Master has not reincarnated on Earth since this incarnation but continues his work.

Joseph, the earthly father of Jesus, never left his son. Joseph left his body when Jesus was twelve. In astral form and in constant communication with Jesus, he escorted and led Jesus to Egypt to study reiki, and then to India to study for eighteen years with the master of masters Mahavatar Babaji. Upon completion of his training with Babaji, he was completely purified or christened. He then returned home as a fully realized Master.

Because of his mastery of purification, when needed, two of the most powerful beings in existence, **Archangel Michael** and his earthly father, **Saint Joseph** (who is Master R or Saint Germain), would literally work through him when Jesus performed miracles and healings. There was nothing Jesus could not do because of the infinitely powerful trinity of himself, Michael, and Saint Germain operating in perfect unity as Jesus. This same trinity occurred in multiple incarnations of Master Sananda, as needed.

Lady Master Magda or **Mary Magdalene** is also an Ascended Master from the same Higher Self as Jesus. They are true soulmates, and they had many children together.

Krishna is an Ascended Master who is deeply part of the conception and inception of Hinduism. He's a popular Indian Avatar that plays a major role in the Bhagavad Gita, which is a transcendent work that metaphorically describes how one might win the battle over the lower consciousness, or ego/mind/identity (EMI), to be within the physical but not of the physical, and to ascend the frequencies.

Kuthumi is an Ascended Master known as a Master of compassion and wisdom. He was Pythagoras, Balthazar, and Saint Francis of Assisi. He has a very high vibrational quality of sentience. He is true world teacher like Buddha, Christ, and Saint Germain.

Mahavatar Babaji is an Ascended Master of such luminosity, power, love, and wisdom that he is the Master of Masters. The teacher of teachers. He materializes and dematerializes his human form at will. He is the true "deathless guru" because he was born in 203 AD, but his human form stays forever young and never gets ill.

He works in background of this shared Oneness and has taught all the other Ascended Masters. He created "kriya yoga" as a gateway to enlightenment. He is the true Hindu Master and the greatest avatar to walk this Earth. He was the guru of Lahiri Mahasaya, who was the guru of Sri Yukteswar, who was the guru of Paramahansa Yogananda. He was also one of the three wisemen who appeared at the time of Jesus.

Babaji's sister **Mataji** is an Ascended Master incarnation from the same Higher Self as Babaji, which makes them true soul mates. Both Babaji and Mataji, along with other beings were the ones in charge of creating the human form and starting the evolutionary cycle for humanity.

Elijah is an Ascended Master whose incarnations include Mohammed, Archangel Raphael, Novalis (the German poet), and **John the Baptist.** The incarnation of John the Baptist helped pave the way for Jesus by cleansing and priming the energies of the world. The title "Baptist" refers to being baptized, cleansed, or purified, so there are no blockages in terms of Self-realization and communication with the greater reality.

Note: **Lady Master Nada** is also an Ascended Master from the same Higher Self and is therefore the female version of Elijah.

Gautama Buddha is the Master of Wisdom and Compassion. He is an avatar of the highest order. He was Thoth, the creator and ruler of Atlantis who lived for well over 40,000 years. He was later still known as Thoth, the Egyptian God. He was also Hermes, the Greek God, as well as Hermes Trismegistus, a contemporary of Moses, also an Ascended Master. Hermes Trismegistus translates as "Hemes thrice great" or "Hermes the great the great the great." The seven principles of hermeticism was authored by this majestic being. This being does a lot of work off world with Master R or Saint Germain.

Djwhal Khul (Master DK) was reincarnated as the "Tibetan Master" when he along with Master R/Saint Germain and El Moriya all left Atlantis as it was falling. He has done a lot of work in India and the Himalayas and is part of the lineage of Hindu Masters. **Lady Master Leto** is the female version of Master DK and both do a lot of work with Saint Germain. Lady Master Leto was just incarnate as Alice Beulah (Schutz) Booras, who adopted the pen name A. D. K. LUK and channeled El Morya and other Masters captured in her books. Alice left her body in 1994.

Paramahansa Yogananda is an uncreated creation of pure absolute or om. He is the Master of Love and rarely incarnates. He was also William the Conqueror. He prefers to work behind the scenes to maintain his level of purity and detachment. Very quietly and in near total anonymity, he was the right-hand man of Saint Germain during Saint Germain's incarnation. They formed an unstoppable team. Master Yogananda is part of the lineage of true Hindu Masters and has worked with Babaji, El Morya, Krishna, and of course, Saint Germain.

On a personal note, "Prayer at Dawn" by Master Paramahansa Yogananda, in his voice, is the most powerful and transcendent prayer I have ever heard.

Saint Germain or Master R is a very popular Ascended Master and perhaps the most prolific. He is associated with the Seventh Ray, also called the Violet Ray or Purple Flame. He is the Master of Energy, Healing, and is known as the Lord of Alchemy. His leaving Atlantis and subsequent pilgrimage to Tibet is what made that area the spiritual center of the earth. It was at this time, Saint Germain created the healing system we know as reiki. At the time, there were 432 symbols for healing that have now been reduced to four due to misuse.

Upon the completion of Christ's work on this planet (Saint Germain was Christ's earthly father Saint Joseph), Master R or Saint Germain has agreed to usher in "The Wisdom That Transcends Knowledge" to expand humanity's consciousness so it can ascend the frequencies and evolve with the greatest efficacy.

The Higher Self or Totality that is associated with Saint Germain is also associated with **Lady Master Portia.** They're the *same* Ascended Master because they're from the same Higher Self.

Master R's incarnations include but are not limited to Plato, Moses, Merlin the Great, Sir Francis Bacon (the real author of Shakespeare), Saint Germain, Joseph the father of Christ, High Priest of Atlantis, High Priest of Lemuria, Amelia Earhart (as a walk-in later in her incarnation), Hercules, Cain, Gilgamesh, the Prophet Samuel, Archangel Uriel and many, many others. Master R is the most prolific of the Ascended Masters and works tirelessly with Earth.

Now we can understand from a metaphysical perspective why these majestic beings are so loving, wise, and powerful, even while incarnate here in the third frequency. It's at the seventh frequency that separateness to Oneness is tangible. In that sense, it is that level of wisdom and love that gave birth to all the teachings contained within this book.

Now, gently say to yourself, "May every notion I give birth to bring about the victory of the light."

Timeless Truth 1

We are not the mind/body complex but the eternal Creator Awareness of all experience and non-experience.

What you are existed well before the mind/body was created and will exist well after its demise. You—eternal Creator Awareness—is the I Am. You are the unchanging, unscathed, untouched Creator Awareness of all experience and non-experience. You are immortal, infinite, and limitless. You are beyond all labels, and have no name, image, or form.

You create endlessly for all eternity to learn about your infinite capacity for ever-growing love and timeless wisdom, and thus ultimately know that you are Source/God/Creator as well.

EXERCISE
Accessing Your Expansiveness

Create without judgment. Go to the beach, the forest, the lake, the mountains, or anywhere you can create an experience without allowing the subconscious patterned egoic mind to infiltrate. Experience the creator and unsullied awareness within you directly. Flow as this and do not stop. Become acutely aware of what "you" feel like, your state of being, your vibration, your state of consciousness, your expansiveness, and your joy. Then journal this experience without any judgment.

Chapter 3
Attachments to Freedom

Freedom is not doing whatever you want whenever you want. Freedom is escaping the tyranny of the finite mind and its limiting body consciousness. The lower consciousness, or ego/mind/identity (EMI), is not free.

The EMI is the human character we create due to incarnation into the lower frequencies of the physical universe. Your EMI is a creation—your creation—that is birthed from the Self (the I Am) but is not the Self directly. The EMI perpetually and mindlessly seeks to balance and harmonize its eternal and immutable incompleteness. Freedom is not possible for the subconscious patterned egoic mind. The EMI can only seek the satiation of its programmed and conditioned desires which in turn creates, justifies, reinforces, and perpetuates its own suffering.

Pleasure is trying to relive the past. Pain is trying to escape the future. Through non-thought, past and future disappear. The voice inside your head is the spell you put over your consciousness and therefore your body of energy. By not "spelling" yourself with past and future, you will cease to conjure up your own suffering. Through the normalization of non-thought, your attachments wither and die upon the vine of clarity, calmness, courage, and creativity. Your true nature—freedom—will be tangibly known once again.

Whatever and whomever your energy is attached to is your master. You cease to have any self-control when attachments exist. Whatever you are attached to has control over you. Without self-control there can be no self-discipline. Without self-discipline, there can be no freedom. Without freedom, life lacks individual purpose. Without individual purpose there can be no fulfillment, and subsequently freedom will have no meaning. Releasing attachments and experiencing freedom gives life purpose and meaning.

MEDITATION
Experience Attachments to Freedom

Close your eyes, take a deep breath in through the nose and exhale out the mouth. Repeat this three times.

Pretend your two eyes are not attached to your brain. Command all your energy to return to you just beneath the belly button and above the groin. All cords and attachments are now severed. Imagine what it feels like to have all your energy back within your body. Feel the completeness of total freedom and the massive increase in energetic power.

Now, close your eyes. Imagine what it feels like to have no name, no image, no form. Just pure awareness and limitless power. What does this feel like? All so-called physicality, thoughts, and emotions are mere shadows projected by this invisible, eternal, formless force. Everything is an illusion other than the imageless, nameless, formless creative force that is you.

Journal what this experience is like.

What Do You Know?

Do what you tangibly know to be true and expect no results. Notice the word *tangibly*. Let's delve into that sentence for a moment because it's vital. It's the difference between the petulant child that we mistakenly deify called the intellect and the towering presence of timeless wisdom and unconditional love. Everybody on this planet "thinks" they know the truth through mental machinations via sensory data. Nonsense. The finite conditioned mind knows absolutely nothing.

I'll prove it to you right now. Just ask yourself, "What do I know?" What answer did you get? Nothing. Your fragmented mind knows nothing. Realize how revelatory this is. Sit with this deeply. Mental understanding is a hallucination.

Everything that we perceive to be true will be upended. Absolutely everything that you hold as truth will someday be revealed as wildly inaccurate. This has happened throughout history. Remember when smoking cigarettes was endorsed by doctors? How about the sun revolves around the Earth? Or that we are alone in the universe? Everything that we've ever hung our hat on has been proven false and everything right now that you're hanging your hat on mentally will be proven false. So stop. Don't bother. Surrender. Let it go.

Don't ever forget what I just wrote.

Do what you tangibly know to be true and expect no results. What does that mean? What does *tangibly know to be true* mean? What you tangibly know to be true in your heart. Now look at the end of that sentence, "and expect no results." The ego mind can't grasp tangibility nor the idea of no end. Because it's finite in and of itself. Do what you tangibly know to be true and expect no results. It forces you to be present, powerfully, because there is no past or future.

No longer will you be expecting a result because you are now firmly rooted in the present moment. The fullness—the limitless magic of the mighty I Am—can only be experienced in the now.

"Expect no results" keeps you perpetually creating at the highest level of inspiration. To do what you tangibly know to be true and expect no results, you must be fully here now. You are now deeply anchored in your immense power, unconditional love, and timeless wisdom.

Freedom

If you expect no results, there can be no attachments to a past or a future. Your future is the past. You are now consciously and perpetually in the act of transcendent creation. If you're doing what you tangibly know to be true, you're being true to yourself. You are free from the conditioned mind. If you're doing what you tangibly know to be true—in your heart—you've liberated yourself from what you have been programmed and conditioned to believe in, identify with, obey, and mimic. See the exquisite beauty from attachments to freedom in just that one sentence.

I've said the following next two sentences for eons of time. Freedom is not doing whatever you want, whenever you want. True freedom is escaping the tyranny of the finite mind and limiting body consciousness.

Attachments to freedom. How I long to see this teaching of Self-mastery embodied here on Earth.

The Power of the Spoken Word

Like Spider-man shooting his spider web, when you're attached to anything, it is your energy that you're using to stay attached. Attachments weaken you energetically. The more things that you're attached to and identify with, the weaker you are.

How could you be free and powerful energetically if your energy is attached to something or someone? If you're attached to anything or anyone, how could you possibly be free? How can you love unconditionally and create without limitation if you are already bound energetically?

Say, "I recall all my energy now." Command it. All cords and attachments are now severed when you do that.

Now you must mean it and feel it as you say it. Don't just say, "I recall all my energy now" like you're reading your grocery list. Say it, mean it, feel it. Don't ever just say anything. Every time you speak, you create an energetic contract with the universe. *Abracadabra* literally means "I create as I speak." Connect completely with the vibration of the words.

All cords and attachments are now severed. Imagine what it feels like to have all your energy back within your body—just beneath your belly button and above the groin. Imagine what that feels like to have all the energy back that you've used to stay attached to all the beliefs, roles, concepts, ideologies, experiences, people, to the past, and future. Imagine how powerful and clear-headed you would feel and be if all that energy returned to you now. Feel the completeness, total freedom, and the massive increase in energetic power. I want everyone to feel that way.

You Have No Name, Image, or Form

Now, that you have recalled your energy, close your eyes. Imagine what it feels like to have no name, no image, no form. This is going to really test the EMI. Watch what the finite mind does when you do this.

The EMI is based upon name, image, and form. No name, no image, and no form is what we *really* are. We are light and lite. The human body is a temporary biological garment, a suit that we wear, not what we are. You're the light, the force; you're the sentience inside animating the human suit. Imagine what it feels like to have no name, no image, no form, just awareness and power to create. What does this feel like?

All so-called physicality, thoughts, and emotions are mere shadows projected downstream by this invisible, eternal, formless force. All are projections created by the unawakened mind.

I am reminded of Paramahansa Yogananda when he talked about life being a movie. I think of Plato and his allegory of the cave. In these contexts, people are trapped and transfixed by mere shadow projections. It is not a coincidence that those two beings see things in a similar way. Through my own higher-consciousness exploration, I have discovered that they do a lot of work together. They operate in a similar way. Plato is an incarnation of an Ascended Master.

Yogananda is an incarnation of an Ascended Master. Everything is a temporary illusion other than the imageless, nameless, indomitable formless force that is you.

I implore you to fully dedicate yourself to these teachings of Self-mastery. The reward will be the tangible experience of harnessing yourself properly to experience infinitely more of the I Am. You'll never be the same because these teachings shatter all illusion. Shatters it. And you'll never bother to try to pick back up the broken pieces of your false image. Once you taste the authentic you, everything you built your EMI upon will lose its allure. You'll realize all you've been doing is lying to and confining your infinite I Am.

Holding Intention without Hope of an Outcome

During my class on Self-mastery, a student asked, "RJ, when you say all the energy returned to you, is it really your I Am no longer leaking energy out to the EMI and its attachments?"

I replied, "Yes. Brilliant. That's exactly what I'm saying. You said it better than me. One hundred percent correct."

Remember the I Am has this thing—the biological garment—that it created and that's draped over it. Through identification with the suit, it completely collapses our infinite awareness. Rosicrucianism was birthed from these exact same understandings and level of consciousness. The I Am gives birth to the EMI and physical body. The genetic entity or physical body is attuned to and part of our local low-frequency environment. The I Am is God directly.

This is all about your EMI and silencing it.

What we are discussing doesn't have anything to do with others. There are no others. That's an illusion that we just talked about in the first tenet because of space-time. Space-time gives us relationships through separateness, based upon the subject/object paradigm. It's an illusion. It's not an illusion—it's real—for your finite mind. Your finite mind is born and part of the illusion. It swims in it, lives in it, is created by it, and is part of it. You can transcend it through inner stillness and diligent self-inquiry.

Thinking is the problem because it creates problems. Thinking is not knowing. Thinking creates questions. We then label these machinations as problems and subsequently we leak our energy on seeking answers. Question the questioner and all is revealed. Thinking creates the illusion of time and the delusion of knowledge. Rather than seeking answers to questions born of the unawakened mind, question the authenticity of the questioner.

The truth doesn't require your participation. Lies do.

The only way you can experience yourself is when you're not attached to anything. The only way you can have self-control is if your energy is not attached to anything. The only way you can become Self-realized is if you're not identified with anything. You must work directly as, within, for, and by the self to realize the Self. How can we realize the Self by putting our attention on something other than the Self directly? You can't. How can we understand anything if we don't understand the Self?

During my master class, a student said, "I feel like although I understand these things intellectually, I've never seen anything mystical that would help me break my attachments."

My reply was, "Your character hasn't seen anything because your character is the one that's in the way of 'what is.' Your character is the summation of your attachments and identifications, so of course it cannot see past them. It is them. These teachings and exercises will be the tangible proof that your character is a shadow projection of the I Am and not the I Am directly. Your character is not the one that really experiences these things; your character is the one that prevents the tangible experience of detachment from occurring. Your character is not the truth of what you are or what is. The belief in the authenticity of the character is why so-called problems exist. The character is the problem. The character is merely a shadow cast by the light of the mighty I Am. Does that make sense when I say it that way?"

The student nodded and thanked me for clarifying.

Tell your character, "Get in the backseat and keep your hands to yourself. I don't want to hear a peep. I'm driving!" Take command of the incarnation. Be fully present, which requires no effort because you are presence. Cease analyzing, judging, thinking, and ruminating. All you're doing is shadow boxing.

We must cease to miscreate the past and future through the misuse of our imagination. Thinking is what locks you in time, and there's no way you can experience the timelessness of yourself through thought. This is why meditation—clarity, connectivity, calmness, communion, and courage—is everything.

The Self is meditation. It exists prior to thought, prior to emotion, prior to bodily sensations, prior to the body itself. That's why I teach and share my instantaneous meditation techniques. Without their effortless and immediate efficacy, we flounder with meditation. We must command our energy. Otherwise, we inevitably lock ourselves in the illusion of time and the delusion of knowledge through the insidious and incessant habit of thought.

That's what the teachings of Self-mastery are about. By gaining dominion over the reactionary, fear-based EMI, the suffering of the human condition will be transcended. This is what it means to be in the physical but not of the physical.

The Truth Is Always the Truth

Remember, we are always the I Am. It's just whether we tangibly recognize it or not. When we are not self-aware, we've abdicated control and sovereignty to the who and what that controls your human character.

Your EMI is completely out of control because it is completely controlled. Namely, by your subconscious programming. Our character is highly conditioned through deep brainwashing and subconscious indoctrination. That's why our character feels so limited because the character is completely and utterly controlled through brainwashing, societal conditioning, trauma-based mind control, and a profound lack of self-awareness. My second book, *Change Your*

Mind, is the treasure map for deprogramming your subconscious mind.

Every individual must do the work to turn attachments to freedom. Everyone. If you want to enjoy your Self and everything and everyone here, this is how you do it. It is not complicated. If the process is complicated, then don't bother. The complicated nature is proof it's merely mental machinations, and not Self-mastery. It should be clear, concise, direct, and tangible. That's how you know you're working with the truth.

Speaking of these things opens us up to the infinite possibilities that exist. Free yourself from the prison of the rational thinking mind. Forgo the limiting past and its encroaching future. That is just your programming and brainwashing. It is not you. It's not the mighty I Am.

Intention and Outcomes

During the five-month master class, a student asked if we can hold an intention without making it a goal and not hope for an outcome.

The answer is yes. This truth is part of how I put my paralyzed, disease-riddled, and septic body back together. It's deeply related in terms of what we call manifestation.

Harnessing powerful intention while simultaneously being completely detached from an outcome is essential for immense and transcendent creative power. It seems like an oxymoron, but it's not. I'll use myself as an example. When I was "permanently" paralyzed from the chest down, my supremely focused intention was to walk. I commanded an overwhelming energetic intention to walk, but perpetually remained completely and utterly divorced from an outcome because I was already completely at peace with everything. Eternal inner peace occurs once we are married to the present moment. It is our ability to embody both presence and intention simultaneously that we unleash our true power as a limitless, immortal creator. I was not attached to any kind of outcome. To the ego mind, that seems impossible, and for the ego mind it absolutely is.

The GPS of Intention

It's entirely possible for the unlimited Higher Mind once harnessed properly. Picture the image of the yin-yang and how they meet and touch right in the center. That's the zero-point. You're balancing intention with complete detachment from an outcome by harmonizing One Self through residing in the middle. That is what it means to be at peace while simultaneously unifying desire/intention with Self. That can only occur when we are residing and creating from the Self.

Intention is like setting the GPS to get to the store. Once the GPS is set, you're completely detached from an outcome because you *know* you're going to get there. You stop thinking about it. You are supremely focused on what you need to do from moment to moment during your drive. You are fully engrossed in each moment. There is no attachment to when, how, or anything. Whenever you arrive, it's fine because you already know and therefore at peace. Thus, you remain the creative act to bring about its tangible reality. This is the uninterrupted and undefeatable flow state.

This crystalline clarity and deep distinction are monumentally meaningful. This state of being also has a lot to do with targeted manifestation. The EMI is incapable of functioning in this way. That's because it's the summation of attachments and identifications. It can never be detached from any outcome. It can be fully present.

Instead, set intention and expect no results. What that does is keep you in the act of perpetual, focused creation. That is the optimal way to create without limitation.

Timeless Truth 2

We are sentience given a body of energy that exists within and beyond space-time concurrently.

You are sentience—divine intelligence—that eternally existed well before humanity was created and will exist well after humanity has completed its existence. You (the I Am) are unconditional love and timeless wisdom whose subsets are talents and abilities that are given energy to create utilizing your imagination, the true mind of God. You (sentience given energy to create) are all aspects of your Higher Self, your Totality. You are an aspect of your Higher Self, and your Higher Self is a direct fractal of God.

Your Higher Self or Totality exists well beyond space-time, and you are an aspect/projection of your Higher Self that concurrently exists here within space-time. You are the part of your Higher Self that is having a temporary low-frequency human experience. You (as the I Am) are experiencing the temporary confines of body consciousness within space-time while concurrently your Higher Self lives and resides well beyond and outside of space-time. You are your Higher Self—just less in volume—and it is you. You are here now, and the rest of you (your Higher Self) is outside space-time now and concurrently.

EXERCISE
Recognize Awareness Within and Beyond Time

Stop thinking. Meditate using any of my instantaneous meditation techniques. Realize that in full presence—complete beingness here and now—that you are always aware of your unsullied awareness. That is the concurrent within space-time and outside of it all at once. The little you is the bigger you and vice versa. Fall in love with this knowingness and live this way.

Transcending the Logic

No thought, in and of itself, has any weight or gravitas. Every thought is equal in weightlessness. It is your belief in the authenticity and veracity of the thought, and your subsequent identification to it, that gives it sway and power over your consciousness and your body of energy.

Life itself is a blank canvas for the immortal creator within us all to create. Nothing has any inherent meaning. And it doesn't mean anything that it doesn't mean anything. The question becomes, what meaning are you going to ascribe to that? That is tempting for the grasping mind.

Enlightenment and even Self-mastery is the effortless unending flow within the river of infinite potential. I know the EMI has conceptualized what these exalted states of being and consciousness are like, but I promise you it's filled with joy, laughter, and lightness. It's only the egoic mind that takes itself seriously and therefore removes the very play of life. Those who have worked with me know I joke around all the time. We didn't invent humor, but we can certainly avail ourselves without limit. Joy births the supreme vibration of transcendent creativity.

Exponential growth for every human being is readily available through these teachings and tangible understandings. From my perspective, we're just now starting to tap into some of the extraordinary things that we can do while incarnate, even while within the lower frequencies of the physical universe.

By working with ourselves optimally, we realign ourselves to what we eternally are and therefore tangibly experience our Higher Mind and Higher Self. Thus, transcending the logic and linearity program of the limited lower consciousness mind.

The key to enlightenment, which is Self-realization, and reaching our ultimate potential has nothing to do with thinking, emotionalizing, concepts, beliefs, so-called knowledge, or bodily sensations and modifications. True success is effortless and permanent alignment with our Higher Mind. Total communion and connectivity. Being fully present here and now. When this takes hold, the thinking, rational mind takes its rightful place as a servant to the Higher Mind. This is success, my friends.

Are You Thinking What I'm Not Thinking?

All of you understand every word I'm saying without thinking. Sit with that for a moment. Your entire life is memorized. The subconscious mind takes care of that for you. It memorizes and stores everything. For example, you see a cup and you know how to drink from it. You get in your car and you know how to drive. You know how to wash yourself, feed yourself, and clothe yourself. You know the directions to drive to work, your girlfriend's house, and the petting zoo.

I want you to look at this deeply, because for us to get the most out of ourselves—this life and these teachings—we must be present. Full presence. How is this accomplished? Without effort. Just totally relax and let these teachings fall upon the ears of your heart. From this moment on, you shall no longer quantify your existence by how productive you are. Instead, if you must, quantify your existence by how present you have been throughout the day. How much of the mighty I Am presence have you brought directly, tangibly to every moment?

Do not denigrate these timeless teachings through mentalization. Commune with me as the I Am is the embodiment of the teachings. Mentalization prevents Self-knowledge—gnosis—from blossoming. Let the aroma, the fragrance of the Divine Self, waft up and fill your consciousness. Don't worry about memorization. That's for the patterned subconscious egoic mind.

The Endless Journey to Absolutely Nowhere

There's nowhere to go, nothing to achieve. Nothing to acquire, nothing to become. What you will quickly realize as we work with these teachings, is that they are profoundly simple because they are direct tangible truths. The finite and fragmented mind is downstream of the I Am and therefore complicates everything. These teachings come directly from the Higher Mind of Source/God/Creator. And believe it or not, what is beyond Source/God/Creator.

The only journey we ever actually embark upon once incarnate is internal. For those who dedicate themselves relentlessly and without hesitation, it is possible to realize the greatest truth: no Self. Being able to tangibly experience this and live this way is Self-mastery. That is the hero's journey and the only exploration and discovery that we ever tangibly make. And you never actually go anywhere.

The Ten Stages of Self-Mastery

The universe likes to test you because that's where evolution and growth comes from. Like attracts like. That's metaphysics. Anything else is BS, and when I say *BS*, I mean "belief systems." Metaphysics is the key. It unifies all the higher teachings that we call spirituality and religious doctrine. The inner metaphysics, the journey itself, looks like this and in this order:

Self-betrayal
Self-denial
Self-awareness
Self-acceptance
Self-confidence
Self-control
Self-discipline
Self-destiny
Self-realization
Self-mastery

Your discipline is your destiny. Your limitations begin where your self-discipline ends. Everything reflects your state of consciousness. Your translation of what is is a reflection and in direct correlation with your level of sentient self-awareness. What you perceive within the screen of your consciousness reflects your level of Self-realization. Everything is designed for you to know thy Self.

The entire multiverse is a multi-frequential and multi-dimensional hall of mirrors that acts as an amplifier and mirror for your vibration. Whatever frequency you are broadcasting the universe reflects it, always. That way you learn about yourself as an immortal creator. It's what I call vibrational engineering and I have developed an entire system for consciousness evolution and specifically manifestation in all its forms.

Cymatics is literally the scientific experiment that illustrates this. All this come back to sacred geometric patterns, which are the true building blocks of all form and function. Within supreme states of awareness, you realize it's all patterned of energy.

What We Really Are

Take note that everything we discover has nothing to do with thinking. What do you "think" about that? You are immortal, infinite, and limitless. You have no name, image, or form. You are beyond all labels, understandings, identifications, bodily sensations, theoretical assumptions, and even imagination itself.

We are God. The Mighty I Am is God. When you say I Am that means God is. When you have a glass of water, and look at just one tiny drop, it's still water. That one drop is still water. We are a drop of God.

When I speak about enlightenment and Self-mastery, I mean transcending the limitations associated with being human through identification with the physical form and the machinations of the finite mind. For human beings, the foundation of the EMI is identification with the form factor or the physical body. That misidentification limits you to body consciousness, which means just five senses in the intellect. This locks in your time. That's the full immersion experience of being human. Once you identity with the body, the physical world becomes real.

Now, the truth of what you are is gone. You have just spelled yourself into separation, limitation, and lack. Everything that has a beginning has an ending. Including the incarnation. We are discovering what gives birth to beginnings and endings. That's the path of the Master.

Chapter 4
Disorder to Order

Cultivate inner stillness and silence, as it reveals the intuitive wisdom to perceive and understand the one true reality.

The created constructs of past and future cloud the crystalline clarity of cosmic consciousness. Once the machinations of the finite mind are believed in, attachment to the body follows. With identification to the physical form, we are reduced to limiting body consciousness. With the adoption and immersion into body consciousness, the physical world is born. Now, disorder will forever live within the chaos of your conditioned mind.

To remove disorder born of past and future, one must question the questioner. Your conditioned mind (personhood) is imprisoned within the concepts of time. Only in silence and patience does the flower of wisdom bloom. It is thought that creates the delusion of knowledge and the illusion of time. Meditation (the Self) annihilates the very concept that you are merely human.

Disorder is thought. It is nothing more than electromagnetic interference (EMI) bathed in e-motion. This bathing creates identification and now the body is sufficiently charged to act. The actor who performs these actions is your EMI. Only in silencing the electromagnetic interference will you realize that none of this endless charade is you.

MEDITATION
Move from Disorder to Order

Close your eyes, take a deep breath in through the nose and exhale out the mouth. Repeat this three times.

Say to yourself, "I don't know, and I don't care." This empties both your mental and emotional containers. You can effortlessly maintain total mental clarity and perpetual emotional freedom because this is *I Am*-ness. There is no effort or straining to maintain *I Am*. Disorder turns to order only when you finally give yourself permanent permission to relax mentally and emotionally.

This is how to move from disorder to order. Journal the difference between the qualities of disorder and order.

E-Motion

What is e-motion? Energy in motion is e-motion.

For greater context, let's look at the true order of creation. At the wellspring being and non-being, what sets creativity (evolution) into motion is desire. Desire is the first order of creation. Desire, intention, thought, emotion, action, and behavior. That is the order of creation as I experience it directly.

When I "log" into a human being using my higher intuitive functionality, that is precisely how they operate. Desire and intention are the most powerful frequencies and therefore the most potent to create from. Desire and intention galvanize creation into manifestation.

Thought—not inspiration—is always in context to a previous identification or attachment. You can't think without first having an identification to something. You can only think in terms of what you identify with. You can only process information in relation to what you identify with. See how limiting thought really is. Thought it simply the movement of the past.

Beliefs and the Limitation of Thought

For commonality of language, all concepts, ideologies, roles, and so-called knowledge, we are going to call them all beliefs. Even so-called knowledge is simply a string of justified beliefs, and beliefs are just a string of thoughts. Let's just label them all beliefs. To think, there must first be a belief in place that you already identify yourself with. It doesn't matter what the belief is. None of them are "what is." None. Beliefs are what we use when we don't know. Beliefs are for children. Do you still believe in Santa Claus?

It's time to awaken and know rather than believe. Let's deconstruct this from a higher-consciousness perspective. Pick a belief-based role. I'm a "this" and I'm a "that." That's the charade that you're playing on yourself. The story you tell yourself—the voice inside your head—is the spell you put over yourself by identifying with what comes and goes. The temporary phenomenal world is matrix of low-frequency illusion.

The voice inside your head is the matrix. Your EMI is the matrix. Specifically, the EMI illusory construct born of temporary personhood. It is a belief-based parasite that traps your infinite consciousness and then feeds upon your energy. Metaphysically, that is precisely what is happening. You should see what that actually looks like from a higher-consciousness perspective. You would drop to your knees and literally beg to be freed from this trap.

Beliefs are the misidentified transitory data that drops down frequentially from your lower astral body and into your mental body. Like a slinky going down the stairs. What drops down from the lower astral informs the next frequency band, which is your mental body. All your thoughts are in context to what you have identified yourself with in terms of your beliefs, roles, and ideologies. Once you have a thought, identifying with that thought is the bathing of it with energy in motion, or e-motion.

Identification is the emotionalization with the thought, which occurs through identification to it. The more we identity with the thought, the more we bathe it in e-motion. This creates tremendous sway over our consciousness and body of energy. This is what gives our thoughts such great gravitas—our deep identification to them—and our subsequent bathing of the thought with energy in e-motion.

As we said earlier, all thoughts are equal in weightlessness. They are all like a cloud. It's our identification with them and the subsequent bathing of them in energy in motion (e-motion) is what gives them their weight. We perpetually create our own suffering and delusion while engaging in this pastime.

Now, once the thought has been sufficiently bathed with enough e-motion, the body then becomes electrically charged, and that's when we act. That process is what animates the body. If it's just a fleeting thought and we don't emotionalize over it through identification, the body will not be energized enough to act upon it. It's fascinating to watch.

Once the electricity is running through our body, which is predominately from the misidentification with the information buried deep within our patterned subconscious mind, the societal conditioning, repeated brainwashing, and trauma-based mind control, we emanate a low-frequency and disharmonious vibration not authentic to who or what we really are. Vibration is what dictates the form energy takes.

Because of this misprogramming, we mistakenly, repeatedly, and habitually harness our energy through focused desire and intention by what we have been conditioned to believe is real and true. What we believe in becomes what we think about it and then emotionalize over. At this point, we charge the body and do something about the desire by taking an action. Repetition of the action becomes behavior. That is how you easily and effectively control the human population.

Those who are detached regain their energetic power and their sovereignty. They recognize themselves as sovereign and powerful individuals because of their clear minds. They have free will once again. They have their power back. Those people cannot be controlled, coerced, frightened, or manipulated. They become very dangerous to those who wish to subjugate, torment, control, and depopulate the planet.

Meditation and the Vastness of the Higher Mind

During a Master Class session, a student asked, "Master RJ, using the 'I don't know, and I don't care' instant meditation is so effective. Does this help bring disorder to order?"

I replied, "You got it. When we meditate, it fosters clarity. We close the door to disorder and open the door to order. When you employ any of instantaneous meditation, you're going to realize that the Real You is the door for entrance into the clarity of the Higher Mind. That door can never be permanently closed. You've just been in the wrong room the whole time. You've been in the closet, the limitation program of the conditioned EMI, the whole time. You live in a mansion but you're hanging out inside a closet."

The subconscious patterned egoic mind is the closet.

Timeless Truth 3

The ego/mind/identity (EMI) is a limitation program that runs by thinking and not the Self directly.

As was explained earlier, the EMI is the human character we create due to incarnation into the lower frequencies of the physical universe. Your EMI is a creation that is birthed from the Self (the *I Am*) but is not the Self directly. This explains why you are aware of everything your EMI experiences and creates. Every thought, emotion, action, experience, and behavior you are aware of. You are the awareness of everything and not what you are aware of. You are the awareness of your physical body and every bodily sensation. That pure awareness (not the judgment and analysis of it) is the Self directly, the I Am.

Just like Source/God/Creator (and we are an indirect fractal of Source/God/Creator) the Self (I Am) holds no judgment. The I Am is pure imagination born of the eternal wellspring of unconditional love and timeless wisdom. It is your EMI that imprisons your love and inverts it into a perpetual state of self-judgment, non-acceptance, and suffering…through thinking. The I Am imagines through love and wisdom. The EMI imprisons itself through self-doubt and self-criticism. By thinking, the EMI traps itself in a past and future.

The EMI is always in direct proportion to the love you withhold from yourself. This lack of love is tangibly produced and experienced through the harsh inner critic—the voice inside your head. Thoughts. Your thoughts are based upon what your EMI is built from and identifies itself with, starting with the physical body. It further grows based upon what your five senses perceive, such as beliefs, concepts, experiences, ideologies, so-called knowledge, and feelings that you choose to misidentify your I Am with.

EXERCISE
Seeing the I Am

Look in the mirror. Do not judge, label, categorize, or analyze yourself. In that pure awareness state, discover who is really looking through your eyes when there is no judgment. Journal who/what is doing the seeing. Write about the qualities of the who/what that looks through the eyes on non-judgment. What does this feel like to see your I AM in this way?

Chapter 5
Ignorance to Wisdom

Imagination through inspiration for the betterment of all is the highest use of the creative force. The reason your mind wants more and more information is because it doesn't know anything. It's eternally bankrupt of Self-knowledge. The mind forever and fecklessly attempts to balance its total ignorance with information. It does this out of fear to have something to cling to. Fear (ignorance of Self) is caused by identification with electromagnetic interference and can only germinate in the absence of the divine.

Wisdom flows on the river of intuition. Ignorance (fear) blocks the tangible recognition of your true vibration. This prevents the flow and integration of your Higher Mind (in the form of intuitive wisdom and limitless imagination) into the incarnation. Ignorance cannot be overcome with the intellect. They are both prisoners, held within the confines of the conditioned mind.

Only by replacing ignorance (the fear-based habituation of thinking) with pure I Am will ignorance die. What blooms in the silence and patience of self-awareness is wisdom. It will flow unabated when there is no electromagnetic interference blocking its signal. Alignment with your own Higher Mind turns ignorance into wisdom.

MEDITATION
Move from Ignorance to Wisdom

Close your eyes, take a deep breath in through the nose and exhale out the mouth. Repeat this three times.

Ask yourself a question that you do not know the answer to, nor do you care what the answer is. This exercise engenders the "no mind no attachment state." Stay in this state of clarity and peace by granting yourself permission to not know or care about anything right now. Let all your mental and emotional energies dissipate.

Now, begin to realize that without believing in the weight or authenticity of any question or the questioner, knowing will flow through you without effort. Without trying to figure out through mentalization, allow your intuitive wisdom to speak, not with words but with knowingness.

This is how to go from ignorance to wisdom.

One Concrete Reality

All the tenets of Self-mastery are incredibly simple and tangible. Only the finite mind complicates things due to its incompleteness. It can only produce theoretical assumptions born of the agitated and limited mind. The Higher Mind is clarity, calmness, connectivity, and communion, and it engenders courage. And that's the one concrete reality. That is "what is."

Everything the EMI produces takes you farther and farther out of alignment. It's not the questions, it's the questioner. Questions will endlessly come if the questioner remains seated at the table. The questions won't stop. By not believing in the authenticity, not just of the question, by saying, "I don't know, and I don't care" but more importantly, "I don't believe in the authenticity of the questioner."

All questions come from the egoic mind. All the questions in the world and their subsequent answers are pointless. They are both born of the same illusion, the EMI. These teachings are discoveries regarding the Immortal Self. They are worth the expenditure of your most precious resource: your energy.

World Culture Is Controlled Agenda

World culture puts the intellect along with memorization of sanitized information on a pedestal. It glorifies the dissecting, fragmentation, and compartmentalization of what is eternally whole as a virtue. Do we know why that's done? It removes God from the equation. It permanently removes you from the deeper truth regarding all existence. The human intellect (the imprisoned mind) can never provide a tangible felt-sense knowingness of the I am. It is easily and endlessly controlled and manipulated based upon what information, misinformation, and disinformation is made available through the five senses. This is perception management and leaves humanity forever uneasy and unsure as to what the real truth is.

That is why the intellect is deified. It's easily poisoned, manipulated, and controlled because it's only fed through the extremely limited bandwidth of physical sensory perceptions. If you control what's fed to the five physical senses, you control everyone's finite mind, but not your Higher Mind. This is why we must go beyond body consciousness.

Seeing Beyond the Veil of Illusion

Have you ever seen the beginning of a 3D movie? You have your 3D glasses on, and they do that countdown with the numerals 10, 9, 8, 7 flying toward you to confirm the 3D aspect is working. That is very similar to how I experience what exists beyond the veil of the five senses and the egoic mind. It is what's going on behind the sensory realm that gives birth to physical reality.

There's a layer behind every layer and each layer gives birth to the layers that follows it, and so on. They all inform one another, constantly intermingling. The key is being able to see or intuit using the Higher Mind.

We are learning how to pierce the veil of sensory realm to see the one true concrete reality that has given birth to all these different layers. Only the Higher Mind can do that. Body consciousness can never do that. The body is attuned to and part of the local environment. The lowest frequencies of the physical universe and its physical sensory perceptions only operate within the narrowest of those bandwidths.

What gives birth to everything and everyone here cannot be tangibly experienced via body consciousness, and therefore, never tangibly understood while your awareness is confined to the local environment. You can never experience the one true concrete reality through body consciousness. Subsequently, eternal truth and timeless wisdom will forever remain well beyond the grasping and infantile intellect. By deifying body consciousness and the intellect, you ensure the entire species will remain imprisoned by physical reality and materialism. When I reference materialism, I'm referring to the concept that objects serve as a primary source of happiness, success, and fulfillment.

The Luciferian Agenda

Once materialism has been adopted, nihilism will soon follow. Now the pathway has been paved for the ultimate agenda: the acceptance and indoctrination of Luciferianism. Essentially, Luciferianism is the indulging in all things low frequency. Its depravity is fueled by a belief that they can somehow avoid negative energetic consequences through the revelation method—that is, if they announce what they plan on doing, they are somehow warded against negativity and misfortune, "canceling out" any negative consequences, so to speak.

"They" are those who desire to rule over and control humanity. It is a non-human intelligence that employs various methods in a desperate attempt at remaining relevant. As we evolve and ascend the frequencies, they become irrelevant in regard to our timeline. And that, my friends, is what you are experiencing: a battle over disparate timelines.

Source/God/Creator has shown me that many have gravely misunderstood the law of cause and effect with the Buddhist idea of karma. Karma, in the Buddhist tradition, is instead a more neutral or natural law where practitioners are asked to think about how best to use the inevitable energy (karma) we create. To avoid co-opting

Buddhists' already-established spiritual terms for our inaccurate definition, we should replace the word *karma* with the word *energy*, or in this case, *negative energy*. These non-human intelligences have created an amount of negative energy that cannot be measured through their addictions. That will take eons of time to work out, which is why they will try anything, such as resetting civilizations, in order not to.

The law of cause and effect is different and eternally in play. Whatever notion we give birth to, we must eventually be on the receiving end of that emanation in order to know ourselves completely as the immortal creator that we all are. The only acts beyond the law of cause and effect are those of unconditional love.

Luciferianism (from a higher-consciousness perspective) lacks any and all metaphysical maturity and therefore real depth. Its main lynchpin is that it operates beyond worldly concerns because of its low-level understandings and therefore its infatuation and attachment to the low frequencies. Luciferniasm refuses to acknowledge and accept, and therefore it must reject—like a teenager's tantrum born of the refusal to grow up—its own evolutionary progression. The teachings and wisdom in my books and courses are the kryptonite (the death blow) for all low-frequency agendas.

Intuition Is the Key to Decoding Intentions

In general, whatever you tell those who are controlled by their EMI, they'll believe. They have to because it's too big a blow to their false identity to contemplate objectively. Whatever you show them, they'll believe. Because they lack detachment, they have not developed their inner guidance system. Therefore, they have no mechanism of discernment through their own inner knowingness, no way of decoding the shadows projected onto the cave wall.

In other words, they will be and behave in an epically ignorant and highly predictable way. Not just ignorant and predictable, but horribly mistaken, tragically misguided, and fatally unawakened. It has never been survival of the fittest; it has always been the thriving of the most conscious.

The discoveries of the mighty I Am through Self-mastery will remain with you. Knowledge of self is the only real knowledge. You are the Self. Gnosis is forever. Concepts, ideologies, roles, beliefs, and experiences—even incarnations—they all come and go. The Ancients called this *maya*. This type of phenomena is contextual. Maya is meaningless except for the meaning you ascribe to them.

Knowledge of Self is everything. Dedicate yourself to the teachings of Self-mastery. Dedicate yourself to your pristine inner stillness and silence. Don't capitulate and allow your EMI to justify denying your exquisite inner nature for anything. It's never worth it.

Timeless Truth 4

The Self (I Am) is already perfect, whole, and complete, and remains changeless through happiness, misery, life, and death.

The Self is not touched, affected, sullied, or harmed regardless of all experience. That is because I Am is beyond all experience. You (I Am) create experiences to understand, know, and learn about the limitless depth and capability of what you really are. All experience is simply the play of your own imagination, which is ultimately the Higher Mind of Source/God/Creator learning about itself through you.

The I Am evolves through the tangible accruing of more and more of what it already and always is: love and wisdom. Through experience, your reservoir of unconditional love and timeless wisdom (sentience) deepens. As this occurs, your heart softens and your will strengthens. Concurrently, the energy you are given and learn to commandeer increases. Evolution is the accrual of love and wisdom, and along with it, you literally become more and more powerful.

EXERCISE
Finding Unbreakable Security

Imagine the worst natural disaster possible. Imagine it goes on for days, weeks, months, years, decades, even lifetimes. Now look at the sun. Would the worst weather, for eons of time, even touch the sun? You (the I Am) are the sun. No matter what happens to mind/body, good or bad, it never actually touches you. Ever. Feel what that ultimate, eternal, and unbreakable security feels like. Let that feeling permeate your entire mind, body, and soul. Stay that way until it is permanent. Journal what this feels like.

Chapter 6
Violence to Kindness

See yourself in all beings and know that there is no need to renounce, covet, or destroy.

Thought rips apart the fabric of what is eternally whole and complete, starting with yourself. Beliefs and concepts are simply a string of thoughts. With every thought you identify yourself with, you take yourself further and further out of alignment. Once you have committed this violence unto yourself, you then do this to everyone and everything.

You must first deceive yourself to deceive others. You are first aggressive with yourself—in the form of beliefs, concepts, and ideologies—which then serve as the justification for aggression inflicted upon others. All physical and emotional harm first begins as an idea in the thought realm. Self-talk is the quiet injustice we inflict upon ourselves which always precedes and is used as justification for the atrocities we commit upon so-called others.

There are no others. All forms of separation are harmful. The lower conditioned mind cannot see nor understand what it is doing. Only by residing in and experiencing what exists prior to thought does one foment the ability to transmute violence into kindness.

MEDITATION
Transmute Violence into Kindness

Close your eyes. Take a deep breath in through the nose, and exhale out the mouth. Repeat this three times.

Imagine that your head is simply a periscope, just pure perception sans analysis. The captain (you) who looks through the periscope is way down deep in the hull of the ship, between your heart and spine. Experience yourself and the projected outside world through this analogy. Resist the habituation of your conditioned mind to analyze and judge anything you perceive.

As you marinate within this awareness, allow your sense of self to extend outward to everything you perceive. What you perceive is simply an outward projection that comes from within you. As you sit with this, you will begin to realize that everything is you. See yourself in everyone and everything.

This is how you transmute violence into kindness.

Cities and the Astral Realms

I've lived many places. Over twenty locations, including New York City, Santa Fe, Kauai, Berlin, Chicago, San Diego, upstate New York, Colorado, Seattle, Spain, and Arkansas. I stay in the location for a little while, raise the frequency, and then move on.

I have found it is infinitely harder on a multitude of levels to live in a city. Any densely populated area combined with an absence of nature produces a low-frequency environment. Where there's more people, the frequency is always lower. That's due to the programmed, parasitical, belief-based EMI.

Whether people realize this or not, part of what makes city living so toxic and disharmonious is the extra thick localized astral realms. Because of humanity's current disconnected state, we incessantly and perpetually infuse the astral with our deep-rooted beliefs and fears. We are literally feeding the astral disharmonious energy. The astral realm is highly unstable for this very reason, and we keep altering it by adding to it, based upon our deep belief in things. If all of us believe in the same thing, whether true or imagined, those like energies come together, and it literally manifests and becomes real.

My wife and I were just in a large city (that will remain nameless) for business. Very nice people, great food, but feeling that especially sticky astral realm was challenging. It's because of the way that human beings typically operate. I kept feeling incredibly dirty and it wasn't correlated to me being outside. Even when I was in a very nice hotel, I felt tainted and sullied.

One way we can counteract this is to maintain the tangible felt-sense knowingness that we are a supremely high-frequency being simply visiting Earth. This tangible knowingness will engender detachment and allow our higher vibration to keep us operating above the dense environment. Almost like we are in a bubble of high frequency and we move about unaffected by the local environment.

Question about Anger

"Master RJ, my daughter has been in a very toxic environment at school. We keep trying to take the high road, but I found myself last night sitting there and just feeling so angry," a student began during a master class session. "When it happens to someone you love, and it feels like emotional abuse toward your loved one, that's where I get hung up. We can't just walk away. We must stay in this environment and see it through, so I was just curious if you could comment on that."

I thought for a moment and answered, "The short answer is: don't take anything personally. That flaming that you're feeling, that's your EMI. Now, that EMI is identified with a role that you're playing called mom. That's what is occurring. That is neither good nor bad. I am simply letting you know what is there in terms of metaphysics. It is your attachment to the role of mom, and the flaming is taking something personally as it relates to your role. It is your personhood that is inflamed in connection to the role that you're identifying with."

Hopefully, that's helpful for all readers. Don't take anything personally. That only increases and reinforces personhood, not the tangible recognition and unfurling of the limitless Self. Depersonalize it. The anger will cease, and the best course of action will be known.

Embrace All Obstacles

Challenges, such as that student experienced, strengthen our will. Not when everything is rainbows and peach fuzz. It is difficult when people are rude and nasty and violent toward one another. Especially when it involves children. But the key is not to take it personally and to stay above it. Note that I did not say don't act. I said stay above it and respond accordingly.

The image I always picture is of a glass of water and oil. You pour oil in there, and the oil rests atop the water. It never submerges. It never drops down and mixes. It never intermingles itself with the water even though it's in the exact same environment. It remains above. It's not affected by what's going on even though it's in the exact same environment as the water. That's the big you rising above and conquering the little you.

Judgment says everything about the one doing the judging and nothing about what is being judged. The need to tell somebody off is your EMI. The need to be right is your EMI. The need for validation is your EMI. The need for justice is your EMI. Even grief. That gets a little harder to rise above, but it's still true. Don't take it personally.

Every time we don't take something personally, what's happening is the Real You (the Self) is present and that presence transmutes and alchemizes your EMI's low-frequency disharmony. The EMI has no control while the I Am is in control. The EMI takes everything personally. I don't like that; I like that. That's good; that's bad. It should be like this; it shouldn't be like that. Endlessly the egoic mind does this. That is your programming on a loop.

The Real You takes nothing personally because it is beyond personhood. Just as the oil that rests atop the water and stays above it all. Remember, whatever notion we give birth to, whatever words we say, emotions we express, physical actions we perform, we are simply revealing ourselves.

The Only Game Being Played Is Self-Mastery

Remember that it is always about Self-mastery, and Self-mastery has nothing to do with anyone but you. Self-mastery is not a moving target that lies outside of yourself. There is nothing outside the Self. Through these teachings, you will develop the self-awareness, self-control, and self-discipline to tangibly recognize the difference between reacting and responding. The only way to do that is to be detached or disengaged from the subconscious patterned egoic mind. If you're not detached, you won't have the clarity between over-reacting and responding properly.

Remember, the EMI is your justification for everything. As you work with yourself optimally, you will address things with restraint, compassion, clarity, power, and courage. Just keep working in that direction.

Can we lose our temper sometimes? Or get carried away? Yes, and that's okay. We want that reaction to be a momentary flare-up, as opposed to a normal state of being. Instead of meditating for thirty minutes a day and the other 23.5 hours, we are disharmonious and out of control, Self-mastery is the opposite. It gives us dominion over the lower consciousness and body of energy 23.5 hours out of the day. If we have a brief flare-up, that's okay. Self-mastery eliminates the perpetual suffering of personhood and affords one the ability to autocorrect on the fly.

Timeless Truth 5

The True Self (I Am) is eternal awareness and can only be directly experienced through the cessation of sensory analysis.

The I Am exists before the mind/body complex. Through incarnation into the lower frequencies of the physical universe, the EMI is created through identification with personhood. That creation, directed by the subconscious patterned egoic mind, is what analyzes and judges.

It is only through detachment supported through meditation that one begins to experience the quieting of the egoic mind and bodily sensations. Inner stillness and silence allow awareness to reside and dwell within its source point: the I Am. Normalizing this state is liberation from the tyranny of the ego mind and the only true measure of success.

EXERCISE
No Puppeteer

Imagine that you are a puppet with no brain and no bones but there is no puppeteer. There is only an unseen force, an energy, moving through you and animating your body, making your heart beat, your lungs breathe, and your eyes see. Journal what this feels like.

Being Fully Present

As we discovered earlier, we are within space-time and beyond space-time, concurrently. That is because we are an aspect of our Higher Self. Our Higher Self is what we really are. The Higher Self exists outside of space-time, and you, an aspect of your Higher Self, exists within space-time. Through these teachings we realign ourselves to what we eternally are and therefore tangibly experience our Higher Mind and Higher Self.

The mind/body complex (the physical vehicle) is a temporary suit that houses divinity. The key to enlightenment and reaching our ultimate potential has nothing to do with thinking, concepts, beliefs, roles, or so-called knowledge. It is the effortless and permanent alignment with our Higher Mind. Total communion. Being fully present here now. Once this state is normalized, the thinking rational mind takes its rightful place as a servant to the Higher Mind. This is success, my friends.

You are Eternally Whole, Perfect, and Complete

The journey begins with the false self to the True Self, to the Oneself, to no Self. Being able to tangibly experience this and live this way is

Self-mastery. That is the hero's journey and the only exploration and discovery that is ever tangibly made. Take note that everything we discover has nothing to do with thinking. Nothing.

You are immortal, infinite, and limitless. You have no name, image, or form. You are beyond all labels, theoretical assumptions, and even imagination itself.

We are God. The Mighty I Am is God. When you say I Am that means God is. When you have a glass of water, and then look at just one drop, it is still water. That one drop is still water. We are a dropper of God.

When we speak about enlightenment and Self-mastery, I mean transcending the limitations associated with being human through identification with the physical form and lower consciousness. For human beings, the foundation of the EMI is identification with the form factor or the suit. That reduces you to body consciousness, which means just five senses and the intellect. That's being human. Once you make identification with the body, the physical world becomes real. Spirit is no more, and you have just trapped yourself into limitation, separation, scarcity, and lack.

Everything that has a beginning has an ending. Including the incarnation. We are discovering what gives birth to beginnings and endings. That's mastery.

Awareness Is Not Analysis nor Judgment

Energetically feel into the word *awareness*. Aware. Nowhere in there does it foster judgment, right? Nowhere in awareness does it intrinsically engender analysis. Once we get to analysis (judgment), we are farther and farther downstream from what you really are (I Am, or pure awareness). Remember, woven with the screen of your awareness is your depth of love and wisdom whose subsets are your talents and abilities. No thinking required!

All judgment and analysis, which begins with self-talk, is not you. The voice in your head is not you. You are the awareness of it. And that voice in your head is your societal programming. It's what uses you in order to judge and analyze yourself (stopping your limitless nature) as well as so-called others. There are no others. I hope that makes sense. All judgment is self-judgment, and it is simply the spell of limitation you cast upon everything and everyone.

Remember, Self-mastery begins with false self (judgment) to the True Self. Then to the Oneself within us all, and eventually no self. This is pure flow state, perpetual equilibrium and momentum, eternal knowingness flowing on a river of joyous inspiration and compassion. You can see this as authentic meditation, which is our natural state.

Now, in the beginning to align mind/body permanently with the mighty I Am, we need a dedicated practice fueled with gentle tenacity. We can call this practice meditation. And thankfully, we have our instantaneous meditation techniques. If you have one that you gravitate to, great. If you stand on your head and that permanently stops you from thinking, then stand on your head. Doesn't matter how you return to here and now. It might be difficult to create the life you desire from that position, though.

The key is to allow perpetual presence. We don't want the ego mind identity performing a task (what it calls meditation) and then going back to its personal limitation program. The actor has performed an action (meditation) and now the actor is back. Subsequently, the ego mind identity pats itself on the back. But our goal is to live in this presence of Self-mastery always. It takes work, but everything and anything is possible for the immeasurable I am.

Chapter 7

Resentment to Forgiveness

Make all actions and deeds reflect the victory of compassion over the ill-tempered outer self.

The discordant EMI holds itself and therefore everyone else in contempt—anything and anyone, including ourselves, that does not conform and confine to its set of programmed limitations breeds resentment and condemnation. We experience deep inner resentment in the form of self-talk.

Anyone or anything that operates outside of our self-imposed limitations is resented for not obeying and suffering. Misery does love company as like attracts like. Resentment and condemnation are the preferred currency of exchange between our subconscious patterned egoic minds.

By forgiving and congratulating yourself for not achieving total subservience to your conditioned mind, you will cease to hold resentment toward yourself or anyone else. As you release yourself from misery, all your previous resentment of others will be transmuted into forgiveness. Every notion you give birth to will reflect the inner beauty and geometry of authentic compassion.

MEDITATION
Turn Resentment into Forgiveness

Close your eyes, take a deep breath in through the nose and exhale out the mouth. Repeat this three times.

Ask yourself, "Who is it that holds resentment?" Your answer will be, "Me. I'm the one who holds resentment." Now ask yourself, "Who am I?"

Your resentment is an illusion just as your human character is. Resentment is the temporary experience of a lack of self-alignment projected outward. Now that you are experiencing the absence of the one who holds resentment, let that space be filled with gratitude for this discovery. Extend that gratitude in the form of forgiveness to everyone and everything your character ever held in resentment.

This is how to move from resentment to forgiveness.

Removing the False "I"

All disharmony comes from disharmonious thought patterns. All thought is in context to an identification and attachment. This means the EMI must already be in place for a thought to even land. Thinking can only occur when the false character is driving the bus of the incarnation. The EMI is the genesis and breeding ground for all resentment. It's the outward projection of your own self-love deficit disorder.

If you really want to know someone, rather than project your own self-love deficit disorder unto them, let them do whatever they want whenever they want. Then you'll see them for who they are. Be completely hands off. That includes the so-called positive actions, such as trying to help, guide, fix, heal, and educate them. It also includes trying to control, chastise, and manipulate them. Just stop all of it, in totality. Be completely hands off.

Try it for one weekend with somebody close to you. You'll see them for who they are. Stop trying to manipulate and control them, even if you "think" it's a positive. "No, these are good things I'm doing." No. Remember, the EMI is the justification for everything. Be completely hands off.

It's a beautiful experience. For me, as soon as the "I" got out of the way, that led to seeing God in everything and everyone. By removing the false "I" there is no judgment. Without that self-judgment projected unto others, there can be no resentment. Now we see all life through the eyes of love and wisdom.

How to Deal with Anger and Non-forgiveness

During my class on Self-mastery, a student spoke up. He said, "Master RJ, I have a big problem with anger and forgiveness. I don't want to get into the details. There was an event that happened in my life that caused me a lot of trouble. This person said that they would do what they did all over again, which infuriated me. I can't get over it."

I replied, "I understand. Let me ask you this question. What would you lose if you gave up anger and your lack of forgiveness? What would you lose if you gave those up? Would you lose the joy in your life? Would you lose the love in your life? The happiness, passion, excitement, completeness, peace? What would you lose if you gave up anger? What great loss would you incur by giving up your anger and resentment? The losses would be monumental. You would lose your stress, anxiety, depression, limiting beliefs, and your inability to move forward. Hmmm..."

The Alchemical Magic of Self-Inquiry

We must look at the one who is holding on. The one who has the problem. My student stated, "I have a big problem with anger and forgiveness." Who is this "I"? Who does holding on to anger serve? What do you receive? What are you feeding and growing within yourself by doing that? What experience are you creating for yourself by holding on to anger and non-forgiveness? Buddha said, "Anger is like picking up a red-hot rock to throw at somebody. You're the one that gets burned."

Remember, everything happens inside you first. When you're angry with someone or you hold resentment, you're doing that to yourself. We must begin to see this clearly. Everything is Self-mastery. The entire multiverse is a multi-frequential, multi-dimensional hall of mirrors designed for Self-mastery. I have traveled everywhere. It's all designed for you to understand yourself completely and utterly. There is nothing else. It's all a projection of the One Self within us all. That's what Self-mastery is. Drop the concept of others and there will be no doubt about this.

Justified Anger Is a Trap

If you weren't so justified in your anger, you would be free. It's not about being right by holding on to anything like anger or resentment. Those are miscreated inner blocks. Let go. Simply look at what you would lose. Imagine how different your life would or could be right now. Now, ask yourself what's stopping you. I know what's stopping you. That "I" at the very first part of the sentence. That's what's stopping you, the false "I." That's what stops everyone because they think that "I" is real.

I like this. I don't like that. I don't understand this. I wish it was like this. I want this. I regret this. I am upset about this. Who's that I? Who is that? Nobody. It's electromagnetic interference. It's literally nobody. There are no musicians in your radio. And there is no "I."

Anger serves a crucial role in human development. It allows us to tangibly feel our individualized level of unrealized expectations. Anger is the feedback loop of non-presence and non-self-awareness. Anger is one of the most potent learning tools we possess because it portends the possibility of greatest harm to ourselves and others. Even when grossly misused, it serves as an accelerant for the evolution of consciousness. Really let that sink in.

Being fully present exudes compassion. Compassion diffuses, overwhelms, and transmutes anger just as wisdom embraces, nourishes, and elevates all understandings. The teachings of authentic Self-mastery will carry you across hurricane waters.

Timeless Truth 6

Existence simply exists to know itself and all its infinite potential.

Existence is just beginning to become self-aware. It endlessly creates endless creations, endlessly, to understand itself fully. Because there is no end or beginning to existence itself, there is only limitless imagination and infinite possibilities. Infinite possible possibilities. The infinite possibility of possible possibilities. You (the I Am) are exactly that.

As you create, you learn about yourself. As you create more fully, more consciously, more self-aware, your creations reflect more of what you eternally and directly are at your core: love, wisdom, and power. Your highest good is everyone's highest good simultaneously and concurrently. This is to know God and to create like a Master of One Self. The One Self within us all.

EXERCISE
Leaving Earthly Desires

Just for today, do not seek anything through physical gratification or mental understandings. Meditate long enough that all earthly desires leave you. The whole, complete, eternal Self will be tangibly known. By journaling, discover what it is that the Self (the I Am) desires.

The Great Shift

By shifting into allowance, you can see completely differently. You'll now allow the infinite possible possibilities to reveal themselves to you instead of accepting and agreeing that something was traumatic and it hurt me. Once you accept and agree to a singular perspective, you are solidifying it. Now it's real. Now there is nothing that can be done. There's no other way to see it. And that's all there is.

Balderdash! (That word cracks me up.)

Acceptance into allowance is alchemy. Does that make sense? This is transformation in real time. You rewrite your past and open the limitless future through shifting from acceptance into allowance. You rewrite the whole thing.

Let me give you a personal example. My own chest-down permanent paralysis. My body being riddled with disease and sepsis, a retracted heart, pancreatitis, thyroiditis, autonomic dysreflexia, type 1 diabetes, and severe auto-immune disease. You are all familiar with the story, right?

I could have easily accepted and agreed with the perspective that this was the most traumatic thing ever, right? My life's over. I can't move my body. Can't feel it. I'm deathly sick. Riddled with disease, and I'm never going to get better. Prognosis is dismal, to say the least. This is beyond traumatic, right? Wrong.

Liberating! It was completely and utterly liberating. It was the opposite of traumatic because that's how I was seeing and experiencing it. I was experiencing it from a state of infinite cosmic consciousness. I had awakened once again! Will I Am shakes the spear of freedom!

It was *not* traumatic. It was liberating. I was free through the destruction of my body. Does that help now that we have the proper framework and context? I easily could have chosen to accept the traumatic perspective. Ugh. Let me start playing the violin for myself.

Are you familiar with that video of me playing that tiny little violin—the self-pity video? That's one way, right? If I would've accepted and agreed that it was traumatic, I could've started playing the violin for myself. How awful. Let me feel sorry for myself and everyone else should too. Please. My last name is Spina, which means "spine." I gave myself this challenge. Nothing can stop me, not even death. And nothing can stop you!

I literally experienced the destruction of my body. It was the opposite of being traumatized. I mean it. I was liberated. Cosmic consciousness had returned once again. The greatest gift and challenge I could have ever given myself was the destruction of my body.

Now, look at one of your traumatic events—so-called traumatic event—and I'm not making light of it. I'm not making light of it at all. Pick a so-called traumatic event, pick more than one, by the way. Choose the ones that are really weighing on you. Choose the ones that are holding you back. Perhaps these experiences are the reason why some of you may have developed chronic mental, emotional, or physical issues that you're dealing with.

Now, apply what we just talked about. Shift it to allowance and see what happens to that so-called trauma.

A student asked, "Master RJ, can you please explain how your body getting destroyed was liberating?"

I replied, "Everything is a gift born of unlimited imagination. Everything. Including the challenges and obstacles we choose to put into our life plan. To lament over our own limitless creativity and unbounded freedom is insane. Self-pity is the single most destructive misuse of our energy possible. It is more poisonous than a cobra. A limitless creator being feeling sorry for itself. Think about that. An immortal, limitless, creator being, feeling sorry for itself."

I will explain more fully how it was liberating. There was no longer any identification or attachment to me being a physical being. I literally couldn't feel my body, and it didn't work. The incarnation was continuing, my consciousness was still having a temporary human experience, but I was expanded by an order of magnitude.

I was fully liberated from identification with the body. I was no longer bound by body consciousness or the human condition. It was destroyed, which freed my consciousness. It wasn't limited to the contraction through identification with the physical body.

My Higher Mind was free. I was free of the story of RJ, the person who went into the hospital, now permanently paralyzed and incredibly sick, and was told he only had forty-eight hours to live. I was now free from that person in totality. I was liberated from the EMI. That whole story of that person was gone in an instant.

I was completely liberated from the spell I had put over myself, the spell of the ego/mind/identity that existed prior to the destruction of my body. I knew tangibly that, the character RJ wasn't me.

I knew it never really was either. It was always just a story I was spelling myself with. And it was gone, literally in totality. And he hasn't returned since. That character ceased to serve my higher purpose any longer. I hope that makes sense.

Chapter 8
Weakness to Strength

Anchor your mind and body in tangible truth and all obstacles, sickness, and disease shall be defeated.

The Soul (sentience given energy) is the cure for all that ails humanity. It is the only eternal and immutable truth. The love and wisdom that created us, when harnessed properly, dismantles and destroys everything other than itself. Complete alignment to that truth allows one to develop an unshakable mind and indomitable will. The further downstream you are from your own love, the weaker you become in mind, body, and spirit.

The finite mind and physical body are part of and attuned to the local low-frequency environment. Without your complete Higher Mind dominion and mastery over the mind/body complex, both will be greatly and easily affected by everything here. If your mind is weak, the body and will must emulate a similar pathetic nature.

Without mind/body being rooted in and attuned to the Self, your human character will personify weakness and succumb to earthly pressures. Strength is unification with Self. With unbreakable mind, body, spirit alignment to your own Higher Self and Higher Mind, nothing can cast its shadow over the light. Sickness and disease will be cast out. Weakness will not and cannot enter the temple of God.

MEDITATION
Move from Weakness to Strength

Close your eyes, take a deep breath in through the nose and exhale out the mouth. Repeat this three times.

Place the tips of your middle and index fingers to the center of your chest. Bring all your awareness and attention to the sensation of touch in the center of your chest. Gently, from inside your chest, reach out and touch your fingertips. This fully opens your heart chakra and fully activates your sentience.

Imagine that your human vehicle and its subsequent EMI are simply avatars controlled and created by the immortal sentience in the center of your chest. Imagine that everything that bothers, frightens, or holds back your human character is all part of a video game and not real. Only the sentience that directs, controls, creates, and is forever untouched by everything is real. Imagine what it feels like knowing that what you are can never be defeated, harmed, or destroyed, ever. Imagine what it feels like to be that powerful and immortal. Now, remove your avatar and play the game directly with nothing in the way of your unbreakable strength and ability to create without limitation.

This is how to move from weakness to strength.

Journal what this feels like to have your avatar removed.

The Perfect, Whole, and Complete True Self

Joy and the laughter are part of the high vibratory nature of the True Self. Spontaneity, being quick to laugh and to have fun, authentically, is the True Self. And not a laugh out of making fun of people. It's the opposite. When it's very easy for you to laugh, to be joyous, to be spontaneous, to be light about everything, the True Self is online. The True Self is immortal. It's perfect, whole, and complete. It literally doesn't have a care in the world.

What does an immortal, whole, complete, and perfect creator being have cause to legitimately worry about? Absolutely nothing.

I've searched the entire multiverse—and even beyond it—and I can't find a single thing. Not. One. You're here to know thy infinite divine Self and share it endlessly.

We are the awareness of everything. The highs, lows, what we call good, bad, right, and wrong. Don't label anything. Don't renounce, covet, or seek. Let it all occur because it needs to. Whatever is happening needs to happen. That's precisely why things happen. So, what do we do in response to the vicissitudes and verisimilitudes we experience upon the raging sea of change? For the biggest, most powerful waves, what is the best course of action? Swim it? Paddle against it? Rush into it? Avoid it?

Surf it, my friends. Just ride it like a surfer. Just go with it while staying above it. You don't have to immerse yourself, sink in, be thrown around, and drowned by the waves. Let the waves occur because they're going to. Just surf it and ride it effortlessly.

Let's go back to our glass of water and oil analogy. When we have a glass of water and we pour some oil into the glass, the oil rests atop the water. It stays above it. It never mixes in and gets submerged, even though it's in the exact same environment as the water. It stays above it all the whole time. That is the nature and one true reality of the I Am. It is such a supremely high frequency, high vibration that eternally stays above everything that occurs here.

The EMI is part of and attuned to the local environment. That false character and its biological spacesuit is what gets completely immersed with what happens here. But what you really are is not. You're not. You are always the awareness of everything. You're above it all, literally. Just feel that.

How to Remove the Avatar

During the master class, I was asked about my statement of removing the avatar. The student wanted more explanation on what that means and how one does that. Here is my reply:

Removing the avatar means to transcend your thinking mind and limiting body consciousness. It is to go beyond the limitations of the finite mind, which is trapped within the confines of logic and linearity and is bound by space-time. It means to remove the identification with the processor that is built upon the narrow bandwidths of body consciousness. Your EMI is literally a fulcrum that is only operational in a completely inauthentic way in relation to what you really are. Removing the avatar is the removal of the one who doesn't know thy Self.

The EMI turns everything into a process of research because it doesn't authentically know anything. It can't see the synchronicities or oneness of things. It doesn't and can never understand the bigger picture. It is always fecklessly trying to figure things out rather than knowing the Self. It can only analyze, judge, compartmentalize, and fragment what is eternally whole. In other words, it is a fool in the most Shakespearean of terms possible.

The character, the avatar that acts as a gigantic buffer between the Real You and the so-called outside world, that's the avatar that must be removed. It produces a runaway freight train of nonstop thinking—none of which are germane to the True Self. The sentience—what you really are—must gain dominion over the avatar (the EMI). We must understand that the sentience is what gives birth to the EMI, but the EMI is a mere temporary creation.

Just as the painter is not the painting. It's in the way of your Self-realization. Your wisdom, unconditional love, and immense power. So, the goal is to see the avatar for what it is: a temporary illusion. This is realized through non-thought. The tangible experience of the Self will come online through the teachings of Self-mastery.

Self-Control and Self-Discipline

How can you create the life that you want if you don't have control over your reactionary finite mind? If you can't control your lower mind, how can you create the life that you want directed by the Higher Mind? If you don't have control over your egoic mind, who or what does? Why do you use your imagination to create scenarios that you don't want to happen? Why do you do that? No self-control.

That is disconnection from the Self (the Higher Mind). It is lack itself through the tangible experience of no self-awareness, no self-control, and no self-discipline. Your discipline is your destiny. Your limitations begin where your self-discipline ends.

Remove the ego mind, which is disharmony itself, and allow pure I Am awareness. Total freedom and sovereignty. Not the avatar, which is the matrix itself. Your EMI is the matrix. You are the matrix. If you don't have control of yourself, the matrix has control of you.

Creating the life you truly desire for yourself is only possible with complete control over the body-mind complex.

Timeless Truth 7

Right and wrong, the past and the future,
real or imagined, life and death are all concepts
and are of no consequence to the Immortal Self.

There is only one moment of creation seen from an infinite number of perspectives. The concept you hold of yourself is a merely single viewpoint within a sea of endless viewpoints. Therefore, it is a singular momentary contraction, a limitation, and only matters to the creator/identifier of the single viewpoint: the temporary human character.

Alter your viewpoint, your perception by expanding your inner understanding, and everything changes even though nothing has changed. You change—the I Am creator creates—and everything changes because you are everything.

You can change one thousand times in a single day and still be wearing the same clothes. The Immortal Self—I Am—does not require self-confining parameters such as mental concepts or a physical vehicle. Your human character is disconnected from the I Am and therefore clings to illusions instead. This is why and how your human character tangibly experiences the concepts of past and future, real or imagined, life and death, separation and lack.

EXERCISE
Shift into Allowance

Take any past event that you have held, accepted, and agreed to from your current level of understanding/viewpoint or fixed reality. Perhaps it's your parents not understanding the way you live your life or a break-up you've had with a partner. Now simply expand and shift into allowance. Allow that moment to simply be just one way the infinite possible possibilities can reveal and express themselves to you. This gives you and the event permission to shift out of a fixed reality and into the spaciousness of the Immortal Self and all its infinite viewpoints. Choose three traumatic events in your life. Journal by applying this shift on how those events now feel/are perceived.

Everyone Must Put in the Work

This supreme and ultimate endeavor—the authentic, enlightened, metaphysics of Self-mastery—is not one that someone goes from the EMI to Buddha with a snap of the fingers. Not even for Buddha. Or Christ or Saint Germain or Yogananda. No one does this.

It's an alchemical process and that is exactly what we doing through these teachings: a dedicated, devoted single point of focus with fervent desire to awaken and liberate oneself from the tyranny of the patterned subconscious egoic mind.

That's been my motivation in every lifetime. As RJ, I would've done anything. I mean it, I would've done anything to wake up. Anything. It doesn't matter because the only point is to fully awaken. To tangibly realize the love, wisdom, and power that we all are. To be it, live it, and share it—is the victory of the light. That's it.

Give yourself permission to go through this transformation. The EMI must die to awaken to what you really are, my friends. The caterpillar must be destroyed for the butterfly to emerge. No matter how advanced, no matter how masterful, saintly, pure, whatever words you want to use, no one does it without the death of the false self. Not even the true Master of the Mystic Arts. Give yourself permission. Just don't get carried away with it. Surf it.

When you transcend the limitations of the patterned subconscious egoic mind, you can recognize and tangibly understand the deepest truths simply by staring at a glass of water with oil resting atop. You see and know at your core the timeless truth in everything. Everything.

Chapter 9
Greed to Generosity

Give and share freely, without fear, and all limitations shall cease to exist.

Greed is a side effect native to the low frequencies of the physical universe. It is birthed by the belief-based parasitical EMI. Its lineage can be traced back to the subject/object paradigm. Greed, once deemed socially acceptable, is ultimately deified through the co-opting and weaponization of competition.

Greed is heavily relied upon and is the primary justified directive within the divide-and-conquer sociopathic playbook. Because the lower frequencies collapse awareness, it engenders the tearing apart and logical compartmentalization and fragmentation of what is eternally whole. Separateness is then experienced internally and externally. This temporary separation from the One Self within us all, causes fear and panic. The finite mind has now birthed the concept of lack.

What ensues is a ferocious and psychopathic tendency to take, accumulate, and hoard at the expense of so-called others. Only by tangibly experiencing the eternal completeness of the self can the parasitical low-frequency programmed EMI be defeated. Whatever notion you give birth to, the multiverse acts as an energetic multiplier. Generosity begets abundance.

MEDITATION
Turn Greed into Generosity

Close your eyes, take a deep breath in through the nose and exhale out the mouth. Repeat this three times.

Pretend your two eyes are not connected to your brain. Imagine that whatever you share freely with others always comes back to you as you need it. Imagine that everything is energy and as you let energy flow through you, you automatically become a larger and larger open conduit of energy, both giving and receiving.

Imagine what this feels like. Imagine what it feels like to be a boundless open conduit for love, joy, and abundance.

Understand that the only block from this exalted state of permanent higher consciousness is your own electromagnetic interference.

This is how to turn greed into generosity.

Journal what it feels like to be a boundless open conduit to give and receive without limitation.

How to Give and Share Freely

Give and share freely without fear and all limitations will cease to exist. Oh, the EMI doesn't like that.

Greed is a side effect native to the low frequencies of the physical universe. It is birthed by the belief-based parasitical EMI. Its lineage can be traced back to the subject/object paradigm. This hallucination birthed the concept of lack and scarcity, which has been used to promote fear.

Give and share freely without fear and all limitations shall cease to exist. See how that's impossible for the EMI. Just that statement, is completely impossible for the EMI to operate that way and still exist. Literally, it can't do it.

As I said, greed is a side effect native to the low frequencies of the physical universe. Higher frequencies afford consciousness a far more expanded and holistic state of being. The Oneness, the true nature of things, is significantly more tangibly apparent. The higher states of consciousness you experience, the more tangible Oneness. Therefore, taking from someone else is taking from you.

Oneness is known while the EMI identity is separation, fragmentation, and compartmentalization personified. It is the opposite. And this is where we go (the lower frequencies of the physical universe) to have this experience.

Where there is no oneness, it's because we universally hallucinate the subject/object paradigm. This creates duality. That is how and why greed is a side effect native to the low frequencies of the physical universe. Higher frequencies, the holistic nature and oneness of life, is tangible.

The Universe Is a Mix of Energy and Sentience

Let the life force flow through you unabated without it being hijacked by the EMI. As you let energy flow through you, you automatically become a larger and larger conduit of energy for both giving and receiving. As an image, imagine a backyard with grass. If you keep cutting across the backyard in the exact same pathway, you wear out the grass. Pretty soon there is only dirt where you have walked repeatedly. Notice that pathway gets bigger and bigger every time you traverse across it.

As you remain present, you become a wider and wider channel for your Higher Mind, which speaks in pure energetics, and you translate it through your intuition. That is the information, the passion, the knowingness, to act upon. All your wisdom, love, knowhow, and power keep increasing and flowing non-stop. This is the flow state of the mighty I Am and it births the superhuman.

The Higher Mind: A Conduit for Powerful Frequencies

The perpetual flow state is living meditation. Being attuned to these higher and more holistic states of consciousness by maintaining perpetual presence (meditation) you literally create a deeper and wider connection to your Higher Mind and therefore the greater reality. After you've done this so many times, like cutting across your backyard along the exact same pathway, you're becoming automatically connected and attuned. And it only increases.

Imagine what this feels like. Becoming a wider and wider conduit of pure energetics. You can relate this to how we see and experience channeling. You just become a conduit for higher frequencies. Instead of having the contracted closed egoic mind that runs by thinking, we do the opposite. We open a larger, more subtle, and powerful energetic pathway by realizing the tangible truth. That we are the infinite I Am.

Our consciousness is literally a conduit through which God experiences and expresses itself. We create the blocks and locks to the totality of all things through body consciousness, which is identification to the patterned subconscious egoic mind. This occurs through the collapse and contraction of consciousness via identification with the activity of thinking. What's the remedy for thought? Meditation.

Meditation seems to work for everything, doesn't it? So does fasting, by the way. That's because what you are really—the Self, the I Am—is meditation. It precedes everything and all is birthed from it. Imagine what it feels like to be a boundless open conduit. A boundless open conduit for love, joy, wisdom, and abundance. What does that feel like? Understand that the only block from this exalted state of permanent higher consciousness is your own electromagnetic interference. Your EMI.

Predatory Energies

A student asked me about predatory energies during the five-month master class. The question was, "Master RJ, when the pathway gets larger and larger and you are open to both giving and receiving, does the direct connection with your Higher Mind protect you from receiving predatory energies?"

I replied, "Everyone, notice the fear that is driving the questioner to ask this question. This is not a judgment or scolding but rather an important observation to take note of. See the correlation between fear and that all questions come from the fear-based egoic mind. All questions come from the doubter, the one who knows nothing. The two main things the EMI gives you is fear and vanity. Don't forget that."

It is fear because it knows death is coming and there is nothing it can do to stop it. It is vanity because it lays claim to and misidentifies itself with all the memorized information. This is done to counterbalance its own total ignorance and therefore has something to hang on to. The intellect tangibly knows absolutely nothing. It is completely and utterly bankrupt.

EMI = Fear and Vanity

Ask yourself, "What do I know?" The answer you get is "nothing." Sit with that for a moment. Realize how profound this is. How life altering this is. The one who you speak with incessantly every day, the one who you are trusting to guide your life, the one who is creating your life knows nothing.

The sheer arrogance of the EMI masquerading its total and complete ignorance. The vanity of the EMI is only equaled by its terror of its own death. With its demise, the I Am is set free. Those are the two main things the EMI gives us: fear and vanity. Join me in freedom and liberation from the tyranny of your mind.

Let me come back to the question about attracting predatory energies. By working properly, you don't attract things that you don't want. You command and magnetically draw unto you what is destined for and aligned with you.

Like attracts like. Opposites do not attract; they complete the oneness or totality of things. These catchphrases that people regurgitate could not be further from absolute truth. *I think, therefore I am.* That's another lie. You exist—the I Am exists—well before you think. I've had to break that completely misleading statement down a thousand times.

The opposite of love is hate, right? That's another popular trope that gets regurgitated ad nauseum. Another complete metaphysical falsehood. The opposite of love is not hate, it's judgment. Don't get me started on these, my friends.

By opening your Higher Mind, you cannot attract predatory energies. Predatory energies cannot align or feed upon our Higher Mind. They feed upon low-frequency energies produced by the EMI and its limiting body consciousness.

Like attracts like. We are a conduit, a vessel, that houses love and wisdom. The summation of all wisdom is unconditional love. And unconditional love is the very wellspring of being and non-being.

When we operate properly through the authentic teachings of Self-mastery, everything we give birth to is whole and complete. In other words, every notion we give birth to will be for the betterment of yourself and everyone simultaneously and concurrently. That has nothing to do with attracting predatory energies.

Sacred Geometry of Patterned Energy

Reiki symbols are derived from sacred geometric patterns. The original reiki, which was a healing system developed hundreds of thousands of years ago by a particular Ascended Master, originally had 432 symbols, which is a magic number in terms of frequency. 432 hz is the harmonic equilibrium of "what is."

The true inception and conception of reiki has to do with deriving these symbols from sacred geometric patterns and then using them for healing. Those precise understandings have been significantly upgraded and expanded upon and they represent the seven steps captured within the Ascend the Frequencies Healing Technique (ATFHT) in my first book *Supercharged Self-Healing*.

All of these teachings come from a deep state of gnosis or Self-knowledge. They will tangibly engender that within you as you perform the meditations. As you dedicate yourself, your quality of life increases. There's less and less electromagnetic interference or EMI. That electromagnetic interference is your poor quality of life—

mentally, emotionally, physically, energetically, economically, spiritually—on every single level. Because that interference is not your true signal. It's not the mighty I Am. It's something you're receiving and aligning yourself with when you limit yourself to body consciousness within the low frequencies of the physical universe.

Electromagnetic Interference = Ego/Mind/Identity

The signals you're receiving that come via physical sensory perceptions are an extremely limited data stream that forms your even more limited intellect. The EMI is not you, it's this place. It is the matrix. You are the matrix. The EMI is AI, true artificial intelligence. The Self-mastery teachings and the ATFHT destroy suffering because they destroy the EMI. They destroy the matrix of inauthenticity: your finite mind.

That direct vibration and frequency of the I Am is the most powerful force. It alters and commands all the layers of creation into perfection and everlasting harmony. By tapping into that, you are at the command center (the miracle machine) of form and function. These teachings are literally birthed from that state. And what exists beyond it.

An Endless Trap That Only Expands

The EMI tries to claw its way out of the darkness, but it can't. It is the darkness. It's trapped within the confines of its own self-imposed limitations. It's like trying to find the kitchen sink in the garage. No matter how hard you look, you can never find it. You cannot find the truth within the ruminations and projections of EMI and limiting body consciousness. You cannot find peace within the eternally disharmonious EMI. You cannot find love, purpose, meaning, joy, compassion, forgiveness, power, or freedom within the prison of your finite mind.

Remember, where you have the most difficulty, the most resistance, is where your exponential growth resides. Where you're most afraid, most constricted, and most tense. The things you have been so sure about that if you investigated it any further—you are convinced you will experience even more pain and suffering. If you weren't so sure of that, you'd be free.

Leave all your pain and suffering here with me. I know what to do with it. Leave it here with me and never pick it up again. Know this: No matter how deep your pain is, no matter how heavy your burden has been, it is not greater than Source/God/Creator's love.

All suffering comes from identification. It is the tangible experience of the collapsing of consciousness and the constriction of your energy. That's what it is but that's not "what is." That is not what you are but rather a temporary created experience. It's a momentary flash within "what is." The EMI is a mere fleeting imposition, a shadow cast upon the cave wall. It only prevents the limitless nature of the Higher Mind, the Higher Self, the mighty I Am to take hold.

How to Transcend the Illusion of Suffering

Wherever you are uncomfortable, sit right there in the awareness of it. Your presence, your towering stillness, alchemizes and transmutes all disharmony. Know the truth. You are the sun. The sun is untouched, unscathed, and unaffected by the weather. What you are—the mighty I Am—is unaffected by whatever goes on with the mind/body. No matter how uncomfortable, painful, sad, angry, wounded, and defeated, the Real You is untouched and unharmed by it all.

Let it happen. Let everything come up. It's supposed to because it doesn't belong to you. When you detox, you're getting rid of everything that makes you unhealthy. That's what we're doing. The authentic teachings of Self-mastery detox you from your suffering, your limitations, your EMI.

Dedicate yourself to the teachings. Don't worry about the mind/body being uncomfortable. Don't make a big deal about it. Don't play the violin for yourself either. Self-pity is the deadliest poison.

Don't indulge in what comes up and it will float away. It'll return to whence it came because it doesn't belong to you. These illusions no longer serve you. It's time for them to go. Connect with me energetically anytime. You know what that means, yes? Just say my name to yourself. You will connect with me. If you get stuck, or you're worried or you're scared, just say my name. Use my presence to liberate yourself.

Use these teachings to free yourself. Just laugh at everything. I mean it. Life really is a joy. If you see life as play, your life will be a joy. It's all playtime to an immortal soul. It's all playtime.

Timeless Truth 8

All forms, whether tangible or intangible are manifestation of Source/God/Creator but to know Source/God/Creator directly, one must remain as one began, unsullied by the tangible or intangible.

I Am is the only absolute, ultimate, and eternal truth. With each notion we give birth not born directly from the purity, majesty, and clarity of I Am; We ease God out. I Am is Source/God/Creator. Any identification we make after "I Am" is untrue, and thus we take ourselves further and further away from the source point of ourselves. We then tangibly suffer our own misperception, misunderstanding, and misidentification.

"I Am (add anything)" is the act of creation itself. The painter is not the painting. Remain unsullied and only be, act, behave, speak as I Am. That state is the direct gateway to Source/God/Creator. There is no experience of the EMI or disharmony as I Am. There can be no discord in non-thought and non-identification. I Am is the door to total clarity, eternal calmness, heightened connectivity, full communion, and unbreakable courage.

EXERCISE
Experiencing Non-thought

Stand in front of a mirror. Use the instantaneous meditation technique of pretending your two physical eyes are not connected to your brain. Experience non-thought. Now repeat the mantra "I Am the conqueror of my mind and body" until this is tangibly experienced and there is no turning back. Journal what you feel like once this is accomplished.

Student Success Story

The following statement is taken from a live class I taught on Self-mastery from July 30, 2022, to November 30, 2022. A student said, "Master RJ, I feel like I'm changing how I see or even categorize things as a problem. They are things that spark desires so that I get to focus on creating the desire into manifestation rather than solving a problem."

I was thrilled. I replied, "That's what I'm talking about. Eventually we're all going to get to the point where the concept of problems no longer exists."

Every moment is an opportunity to create, connect, and commune without limitation. You're already trapped in the closet of the patterned subconscious egoic mind if the very concept of a problem even exists. The finite mind panics because it's bankrupt of tangible truth, and it says, "I need a way, I need a process." No, you don't. Your character does but you don't. The Real You doesn't need anything. You already are everything. But we first must get out of the closet, the subconscious patterned egoic mind. One must get in to get out.

The Self is whole and complete. It's not lacking anything. It doesn't need anything. Need doesn't tangibly or authentically exist. If you don't have it, then you don't need it. If you don't have it right now, then you don't need it. Sit with that for a moment. Need does not exist. Never did. That, my friends, is the fear of lack programmed into your subconscious. Remember, 95 percent of reality creation comes from the subconscious mind. The mind virus of need has been deliberately put into our subconscious mind. Now you know the genesis, the main underpinning, as to why the human race continues to struggle so mightily.

Chapter 10
Limitation to Limitlessness

Align your every desire to the freeing of your mind and body, and the kingdom of heaven shall reign once again.

Desire is the first order of creation. It is also the single most powerful force, from a frequential perspective, that we can directly harness to create consciously. To infuse this realm with true divinity—our unconditional love, timeless wisdom, and indomitable will—we must command, with a single point of focus, the freeing of the mind/body complex from all delusions created through misperceptions, misunderstandings, and misidentifications.

The physical realm is as real and limiting, and always in direct correlation, with your belief in the authenticity that you are the mind/body complex. The inverse of that statement is also true. Tangibly knowing that you are a supremely higher-dimensional energy being having a temporary human experience allows you to directly experience yourself as the divine fractal of God that you are.

The kingdom of heaven is here now. It's you. Your Higher Mind, loving heart, and unbreakable spirit is the kingdom of heaven embodied here and now within physical reality. Only your own ignorance and fear prevents the truth and only your transcendence of them can liberate you.

MEDITATION
Move from Limitation to Limitlessness

Close your eyes, take a deep breath in through the nose and exhale out the mouth. Repeat this three times.

Pretend you just arrived here, no past no future. Sit down, feet planted firmly on the ground, your back straight with your head tilted slightly downward. Close your eyes. Relax your tongue in the back of your mouth like a clam resting in its shell. Place your hands, palms up, on the upper most part of your thighs. Breathe in deeply from your diaphragm and exhale out your nose. Repeat this breathing three times.

Now, with the utmost fervent desire of your soul, repeat the command 'the body is nothing. The body is nothing. The body is nothing.' Do not stop until this eternal truth is tangibly realized and experientially known.

This is how to move from limitation to limitlessness.

Christ and the Ascended Masters

During the Self-mastery class, a student asked if I could expand on the concept of Jesus as a yogi. I was more than happy to!

We probably have different definitions of yogi. A yogi is a Self-realized being, which is one who knows and tangibly understands thyself. This is also what an enlightened being is. Enlightenment and Self-realization are the same thing. Enlightenment and Self-realization are full communion with your Higher Self. You have realized the Self, and you are your Higher Self, just less in volume. Self-realization is full communion and attunement to what you really are, your Higher Self.

The name Christ comes from being purified or christened. This is what it means to be a true yogi. The purification and alignment to the mighty I Am. When Joseph, Christ's earthly father, died, he stayed with Christ in spirit. He guided him to Egypt to study ancient healing modalities such as reiki, which was created by his earthly father eons ago in a different incarnation as Master R, or the being more commonly known as Saint Germain.

Christ's earthly father (in pure spirit form) led him to India, where he eventually studied with the great Master Mahavatar Babaji. After twenty years of being trained in the Mystique Arts, Christ returned as a fully realized Master—a true Yogi just like great Hindu Masters.

Christ is one of the more advanced beings to ever walk the earth. This is probably obvious, but from a purely metaphysical perspective, and being able to see that being, dare I say, know that being, he is truly one of the more advanced beings. A true and authentic timeless teacher of humanity. I love him and know him with all my heart.

To me, what is truly majestic about the being known as Christ, who has had many other incarnations by the way, is the purity that soul was able to achieve. That was a very, very important lifetime. The being known as Christ was also surrounded by Ascended Masters. As I mentioned briefly before, his earthly father, Joseph, is an incarnation of an Ascended Master more commonly known as Saint Germain.

His mother, Mary, is not technically an Ascended Master, but she is just as evolved and operates exactly like one. Christ's partner, Mary Magdalene, is a soulmate of Christ. In other words, Mary Magdalene is also an Ascended Master. She is literally part of Christ's Higher Self.

The three wise men—the being known as Mahavatar Babaji, the being known as Paramahansa Yogananda, and the being known as El Moriya—are all Ascended Masters. They are also all Hindu Masters.

The incarnation—Christ's life—was going to be successful. Period. Nothing was going to stop the success of that incarnation. Absolutely nothing. And the beings that were involved with it—those beings that I just mentioned—I promise you they would've done anything and handled anything to make sure that that incarnation was successful.

Many of the things that are in the Bible are just complete and utter nonsense. And many of the things are also completely and utterly accurate. What strikes me most is that humanity swears by and believes in precisely the things that never actually occurred and completely dismisses as fiction the things that actually did occur.

I'm very well versed with that overall experience and stream of events. Let's leave it at that. Christ was and still is a supreme yogi of the highest order and a true Master of the Mystique Arts. He is not the originator of the Mystique Arts or the Healing Arts, but by truly mastering himself, he became a master of them and could perform them at will.

Timeless Truth 9

All limitations are self-imposed.

Existence is all one. There are no blocks or limitations in "what is." We create blocks of limitation namely through identification with maya, such as beliefs, concepts, ideologies, or so-called knowledge. This occurs due to self-imposed body consciousness (EMI). There is no resistance to anything. Existence is all one. We create resistance and therefore the experience of limitation through identification. We do this incessantly by thinking and emoting.

You are your Higher Mind. You are your Higher Self, just less in total volume. We are a bubble of pure sentient imagination within the Higher Mind of Source/God/Creator. Freedom from the tyranny of the subconscious patterned egoic mind gives you the tangible experience of your true and eternal limitless nature.

Limitations are created by our identification with creations. Creations are not the creator directly. By identifying with any creation, we create our own self-imposed limitation. We are such powerful creators, but we are creating from the subconscious patterned egoic mind. We have yet to consciously create directly from our own perfection and divinity but rather from the self-imposed limitations of the low-frequency logic/linearity paradigm of the reactionary thinking mind.

EXERCISE
Exploring Limitations

What is your highest desire? Write it down. Now write down what holds you back from achieving this and how that feels. Now write down something from your mundane daily to-do list. Now write down what holds you back from achieving this and how that feels.

Deeply examine the feeling or energetic quality between the block you assign to achieving your highest desire and the feeling or energetic block you assign from a mundane chore. Realize the feeling or energetic quality that you assign is actually the only difference between these two things being achieved. The energetic feeling, weight, meaning, or gravitas you assign to the block is the only difference. All limitations are self-imposed.

Student's Transformation Story

During my Self-mastery class a student shared the following story with the class:

> *Well, I have had a thirty-year relationship with antidepressants, and of those thirty years, for twenty-five of them I've been trying to get off them. I grew up in the Northeast and the energy there was not good for me. I'm very sensitive and I didn't know it at the time. I thought something was wrong with me. I thought I was a failure, that I was less than. I grew up, just that kind of thing embedded in me. But I was trying to break the habit of them. So, twenty-five years ago I moved to Wyoming, which was much better for me.*
>
> *But every time I tried, I felt like I was pulled down in a riptide and I was drowning. And again, each time I felt like a failure because I couldn't get off them. Then, I was diagnosed with MS twenty years ago. That did not help with the antidepressants, trying to get off it because my body was starting to deteriorate and decline.*

Through this course and a recent move, everything I look at is different now. I've really worked on letting go of my past and detaching, and it's just a lot easier for me now to not go to my little pill bottle and take that.

And I've been very successful at it. A couple weeks ago I felt like I needed to get back on it a little bit and then I realized, "Wait a minute, I'm like cutting these pills in half and then half of a half and then I'm having more days in between. This is working for me in a way that it never did before."

I'm very excited that I'm getting off this rollercoaster ride and looking at things in a different way and tuning into who I really am instead of my ego mind as much. I'm having more and more control over it. It is a process; it takes a while.

I like what you said, RJ, about you just keeping your body going, so your I Am can come through. I've shifted to that instead of being so focused on my body and every little thing because it's hard to watch your body decline. I can't walk as well as I used to. It's very hard to do that, to have that happen and not have it affect you in a deep way.

But I am looking at things differently and I can see a change and a big shift and really a transformation. I'm very excited about this and… Sorry, it's hard for me to talk about it. But I just feel like I went from weakness to strength, and I continue to go that way and I'm really looking forward to the future and what it holds for me. I can't thank you enough, RJ.

Bravo! There are no words for me to tell you how I feel when people share these kinds of things with me and one another. This is the whole point. It is our quality of life. And as our friend has figured out, she has the power to do this. We all do. We always have. We always will. We are power. This is amazing. Congratulations.

What we are is timeless, limitless, and immortal. The more that you work with the timeless teachings of Self-mastery, the more powerful, loving, and wise you become. And just like our classmate said, it's transformation. It's not change. I am not interested in change! Change implies the residue of the past. I'm interested in transmutation, transformation, and transcendence. That's alchemy. That's magic. And real magic is metaphysics. That's how things really work. Thirty years later and now here she is transcending and transforming. I love it.

Isn't it amazing that by working with the teachings of authentic Self-mastery that transformation in health has been achieved. Thirty years later you have overcome what every medicine and modality that's been pushed your way couldn't. That's because only the truth heals. Only the truth. And the truth is not a pill, a tincture, an antibiotic. I don't care what it is.

When we work with the mighty I Am (the unlimited Self) there are no limitations. None. You must create a limitation. You must buy into one. You must align yourself with something outside the Self. You must adopt a singular point of view. And as soon as you adopt a point of view, your consciousness completely collapses, and your energy constricts. There is no healing in this.

Align yourself to the highest truth and the body must follow suit. Remember, whatever conceptualized reality that we create for ourselves, our body must have the tangible experience of that. That is the mind/body connection in one sentence. A greatly expanded state of consciousness, the body must have the tangible experience of that as well. The teachings of Self-mastery are the truth and the body must follow into healing.

Chapter 11
Complexity to Simplicity

Allow "what is" and simply work with deep inner knowingness birthed by the crystalline clarity of now.

Complexity arises the moment we let fear create the thinking mind. By rejecting the clarity of now, endless simulations of past and future disempower you. Non-stop mental machinations and pointless emotionalizations result in delusion of mind and weakness of will. The thinking mind is the chaos and complexity born of fear. Nestled within the simplicity of now, choiceless detachment throws open the door to your Higher Mind and the tangible recognition of your Immortal Self.

Without the chaos and complexity brought upon by the fear-based reactionary EMI, your own towering and eternal presence would be known. The complexity of doubts and ever-present fears overwhelm the underpinnings of trust and faith inherent within the Self. When firmly anchored within the now, mental complexity born of fear is defeated by the simplicity of truth and presence.

By allowing what is to flow, the non-stop complexity and turmoil inherent in trying to make existence fit the paradigm of your limitation program, simplicity and clarity will be tangibly known. Mental and emotional projections will cease and with it, complexity will turn to simplicity.

MEDITATION
Turn Complexity into Simplicity

Close your eyes, take a deep breath in through the nose and exhale out the mouth. Repeat this three times.

Ask yourself, "Who is it that complicates things?" Your answer will be, "Me. I'm the one who complicates things." Then ask yourself, "Who am I?" You will get no answer because your EMI is simply electromagnetic interference and not you. It is a mere shadow cast upon the eternal light of the I Am.

Now that your mind is clear and your emotions have stabilized, in the exact same way you give yourself permission to relax physically when you sit or lie down, give yourself permission to fully relax mentally and emotionally. Give yourself complete inner stillness, peace, and silence. Fall in love with the exquisite feeling of simplicity that comes with total mental clarity and emotional balance. Make this simplicity, this feeling, the greatest love of your life.

This is how to turn complexity into simplicity.

The Point of Existence

What is the point of existence?

To experience, learn, and evolve. That is the purpose of everything. That is the sole directive of existence itself. To experience, learn, and evolve. To know thyself and all thy infinite potential. Existence exists to deeply experience itself and therefore tangibly understand itself.

Existence does not exist with the directive of becoming mired within a state of non-knowing.

For us, humanity, we tend to get muddled because of duality. That is due to our low-frequency environment. The density of energies collapsing into one another forming height, weight, and width or what we have labeled 3D. Because we are experiencing space-time, we then mistakenly operate within a subject/object paradigm. Space affords the experience of so-called separation through the concept of relationships, not oneness.

We have a temporary experience of individualization—a single unit of consciousness—instead of knowing just a second ago we were all one. This tangible experience of oneness is God Consciousness or God realization. So, when we're here, until you've transcended your egoic finite mind, your EMI, you see and experience yourself as separate. Once that illusion is solidified within your mind, the subject/object paradigm becomes real. This what creates duality. Your suffering, and everyone else's, will be the result.

Duality and Oneness

Through the delusion of duality, we have given birth to the concepts of right and wrong, good and bad. Positive and negative. It's an illusion. We exist within an ocean of compassion and love. Low frequency and high frequency are real. That's metaphysics and tangible. The rest of it (duality) is just a single point of view.

Duality is a possible experience within the limitless possibilities of possible possibilities. That is the reason it exists. Because it's possible. And because it does exist as an experience, it is therefore available to us as an experience. The low frequencies of the physical universe is the only place that you can have this type or quality of experience.

What does an immortal, limitless creator being want? Experience. Every kind of experience, including the experiences of limitation, separation, and duality. Because it's available to you and to know thy Self and all our infinite potential, the challenges associated within the experience of duality and self-imposed limitation is essential. Remember, we leave here with a stronger back and more tender heart, and that, my friends, is the evolution of consciousness.

Timeless Truth 10

We are always waking up to the infinite possible possibilities contained within every single now *while housed within a multi-frequential and multi-dimensional structure.*

Which *now* we experience and inwardly shift to is based upon personal and collective creativity in regards to what we most fervently desire to experience, moment to moment, based upon our level of sentient self-awareness and vibration.

Within every single *now* is the complete, full, and in-depth totality of infinite possibilities. We, sentience (as tangibly experience it), endlessly shift our inner perception and self-understanding. This inner expansion and contraction results in the changes we tangibly experience in the so-called outer world.

Because each soul is unique, we are seeing and experiencing the infinite variety of choices one can make within every single now. As humanity is guided and taught from timeless wisdom and unconditional love, it will begin to tangibly experience these greater aspects and qualities within themselves. This will result in a higher-frequency perspective and choices available. This will subsequently be reflected in the changes we shall see in the so-called outer world.

EXERCISE
Revealing Infinite Possible Possibilities

Look at a situation you feel stuck in and powerless to change. Shift from the state of acceptance and agreement that this is the one and only reality into the state of allowance. Let the infinite possible possibilities reveal themselves within the screen of your consciousness.

Journal what the tangible difference is between acceptance and allowance. Stay in this expanded allowance state of allowance and see what happens to your state of being regarding everything that you previously accepted and agreed to that was discordant to you.

Question on Dreams

"This week, I've been having difficult dreams all with the thread of separation and/or my being in transition, unpacking or packing and feeling a lot of emotional discomfort in my dreams," a student said during my Self-mastery class. They went on, "Through the night I am employing all your [techniques]. I remember once you said that even in your sleep you can master no thought. Can you talk more about these things?"

Consciousness never goes to sleep. Your EMI's interactive experience with this realm is put on pause momentarily, but you're not your finite mind or physical body, which is attuned to and part of this realm. At a certain level of Self-mastery, the mind/body complex goes to sleep, but what you are does not. You're fully aware of everything including the so-called dream state. This place—Earth—is the dream state, by the way. Our so-called waking state is the dream state because of the unawakened EMI.

Dreams can mean a lot of different things and they serve a variety of functions. The dream state is a safe way for you to work things out, so to speak. If you were to work them out in "physical reality," there would be a level of tangible repercussion or energetic cause and effect. In your dream state it is "safe."

Your subconscious is working through a lot of things all the time, bringing up a lot of embedded fears and traumatic experiences, giving you scenarios in which you see yourself working these things out in your dream state. Essentially, the dream state is a safe place in comparison to physical reality.

Let's say you had a very difficult relationship with your mom or dad and there's a lot of non-clarity, tension, and attachment. Having discourse with mom or dad could create severe emotional, mental, or physical disharmony. A plethora of things could be catalyzed if the relationship is combustible. There is nowhere near as much potentiality for harm in the dream state. It's a relatively safe environment comparatively speaking. Now, I'll take that a little further. All realms are a safe environment because you're immortal and what you really are is untouchable.

Your EMI is terrified of death because it knows its clock is ticking. You—what you eternally are—is immortal and divine. So, all realms are, in truth, a safe place. They are a creative event space in which we learn about the immortal limitless Self within us all. There are simply different kinds of consequences within physical reality because we must keep the vehicle intact to continue the physical incarnation.

The EMI Seeks Control Because It's Totally Controlled

Your EMI is pulling out all the stops. It is getting desperate. This course is kryptonite for the EMI. The mighty I Am—once activated through the teachings of Self-mastery—is like the white-hot tip of a burning incense stick. Nothing can withstand its touch.

The EMI will say and do anything—and I mean anything—to keep itself alive. Remember, it cannot live without a host. That host is your finite mind and body of energy.

Only the Truth Heals

Only the truth heals. We think time heals all wounds. It does not. Time doesn't authentically exist. It's the detachment that human beings typically experience through the passing of time. Mistakenly, due to our unawakened state, we attribute the healing to time. But it is only the truth that heals. You've simply become detached. You're no longer attached (identified with) that experience. You've gotten a level of clarity and subsequently were able to let it go. You're experiencing your Self rather than the misperception, misunderstanding, and misidentification to the experience. It is the truth that heals and only the truth that heals.

The I Am Is the Captain and the Body Is the Ship

Sentience, what you really are, sits between your heart and your spine. This is precisely why everyone points to their chest when they indicate themselves and say me. Give yourself eternal and unbreakable permission to just be here now. Nothing but pure presence and unsullied awareness. Now imagine what it feels like to sink so far back into yourself that the mind/body complex requires no effort to engage it.

Because of the progression that you have experienced through these teachings, there are fewer and fewer questions. So, what's happening? The kryptonite is working because all questions come from the egoic mind. The EMI is losing its power over you. There will come a point where you don't have any questions about anything. Ever.

Chapter 12
Anger to Compassion

Operate with non-judgment, and loving communion with all life will be tangibly known.

Anger gives us the tangible depth of EMI identifications that have not been satiated. Anger is always in direct proportion to the energetic strength of attachment and hierarchy of importance we have assigned. The more important we have made something, the bigger the energetic attachment is, the greater the anger we experience.

Anger serves an important role in human development. It allows us to tangibly feel our own level of unrealized expectations. It gives us the exact level of non-presence and non-self-awareness we experience in the moment. Anger is one of the most potent learning tools we possess because it portends the possibility of greatest harm to ourselves and others, even when misused as motivation.

Being fully present is compassion. All of you here now. All your love, forgiveness, and divinity emanate from you when you are fully here. From presence compassion flows. Compassion overwhelms, diffuses, and transmutes anger like wisdom embraces, nourishes, and elevates all it encounters.

MEDITATION
Transmute Anger into Compassion

Close your eyes, take a deep breath in through the nose and exhale out the mouth. Repeat this three times.

Pretend you just arrived here, no past no future. Imagine that what has made you angry was simply a scene in a movie that you watched. The movie has absolutely nothing to do with you. You just watched it, that's it. It was for entertainment purposes only.

Imagine what it feels like to have watched a movie that you enjoyed and learned something from. Now imagine what it feels like to share that joy and useful information with someone, and it helps them. Imagine what it feels like to have what was once your pain but has turned into joy and wisdom help heal and save someone.

This is how to transmute anger into compassion.

Another Health Breakthrough

"I was diagnosed with cancer twenty-five years ago," a student revealed during the Self-Mastery course. "I've had chemotherapy and radiation multiple times since the diagnosis. Ever since I was first told about my cancer, I've had PTSD. That moment, that diagnosis, haunted and terrified me to the point that I couldn't even drive my car anymore. I had to give up my career because of my PTSD. Not the cancer, the PTSD. It has been the most debilitating disease I could have ever imagined. It has taken everything from me. Everything. Not anymore. After twenty-five years, it has finally left me. This course, your teachings, have given me back. I have my life back. I can't thank you enough, RJ. I love you so much."

I love it. Your success is inside you. It is you. Bring it out now through the authentic teachings of Self-mastery. Say it with me and feel every word as you say it, "I Am the immeasurable I Am in full stature now."

It's the tangibility. The tangibility is the key to everything. The learning must be experiential, not informational. We are in a new age.

And it is the age of the Wisdom That Transcends Knowledge. It absolutely is. And this is what we are all doing right now through these teachings. This is what I'm here to do while on Earth and there's nothing that can stop me. Nothing. And there is nothing that can stop you when you work with yourself in this way.

Everything—wisdom, love, power, compassion, courage—is about tangibility. Mental understandings are nothing. There is nothing there. All mentalizations are useless. Truth must be a felt-sense resonance of inner recognition and remembrance. It is embodied not theorized or conceptualized within the lower astral or mental body. Those are delusions of the conditioned finite mind.

Who Is the I That Thinks It Understands?

Let me say it this way. When someone says to me, "Oh, okay, I understand," immediately I know they don't. Your character is telling me. "RJ, I understand what you just said." Nothing has been tangibly recognized within but rather the actor is performing the action of mental processing.

Mental understandings mean you have a frame of reference (the past) that you're now conjuring up that allows you to make a connection now by reliving the past, which you'll then project into a future. It's a limitation program. It's reliving the past as your eternal future.

When you say, "I understand," your EMI (which is built upon past identifications) conjures up a memory that you superimpose onto something I just said now. It's living in the past. Your character is in total control of you. Let what I say land upon the ears of your heart.

The teachings will bring forth a tangible remembering of what you really are. The recognition of Self. That is gnosis. Self-knowledge. That is the only real knowledge that exists. Knowledge of Self. The Self is the only thing that is real, that endures. Everything else simply comes and goes and has nothing to do with you.

The Supreme Intelligence

When you surrender completely to the present moment, you are allowing a supreme intelligence into your life. Only when you operate from the present moment is the head not in the way. The supreme intelligence is your Higher Mind. It is your Higher Self directly. Only in the present moment is your supreme intelligence accessible and online. And when it happens, it's tangible as many of you are now experiencing. This is so far beyond all mental understandings.

Stop trying to understand anything mentally. For the Supreme Intelligence to enter into your life, you must make a switch. Stop trying to mentally understand everything and switch to how present you can be. Watch what happens.

Do not be the warden of your own prison. Whatever you're aligning yourself with is just a single perspective. It is not what is. It's just a perspective, which is a limitation trapped within the parameters of your conditioned mind. A singular perspective is the collapsing of consciousness. Be so present—be so fully here and now—that the tangibility of timeless truth washes over you and bathes you in pristine clarity and full communion.

That is gnosis. That is the evolution of consciousness with the greatest efficacy. That is the supreme quality of life that only the authentic teachings of Self-mastery can engender. Let the supreme intelligence operate your avatar because that supreme intelligence is the Real You.

The Mantra to Liberate the Mighty I Am

"The body is nothing. The body is nothing" is the mantra I used to say repeatedly as a kid. When you start to feel that statement—the finite mind along with the so-called realness of the physical body—begins to evaporate. All the experiences the body has had along with the concepts, beliefs, and limitations born of the egoic mind fall away. Only with identification to the body is the physical world birthed and then becomes real. And then it's solid. Now, you're trapped in body consciousness.

When this body is seen for what it is (energy), you'll start to see the world this way as well. Because it is the truth. This is extremely powerful. How to move from anger to compassion as well as how to move from limitation to limitlessness. That mantra will do exactly that. I can remember doing it a long time ago when I was a kid. That's exactly what I used to do. Word for word.

As you do this, you will experience the tangibility of the body simply existing as energy. Watch how your finite mind disappears through this practice as well.

For me, existence is akin to the play and manipulation of a Rubik's cube. I'm not actually moving or doing. I'm simply bringing the depth of me—the limitless I Am—into the screen of my consciousness. Commanding it.

The I Am is whole and complete. It contains everything. There is an inner shift of recognition which brings into view whatever aspect of the mighty I Am that you desire to tangibly experience and be the awareness of. At a certain point, there is no process to it anymore. It just happens.

The Purpose of "the Body Is Nothing"

During the master class, a student asked the following, "Master RJ, the mantra 'the body is nothing.' I understand it is about not identifying with the body. It is not who I am. So, in repeating *the body is nothing,* is the idea to experience our true self by shifting our focus and self-perception?"

Yes, it is a monumental shift in self-understanding. The so-called physical body is a body of energy that houses what you really are. It's energy, which the mighty I Am commands and manipulates perpetually. There's nothing there. It's energy. Potential. Command and create it as you deem fit.

Let's look a little deeper into this. When you perform the assigned meditation or the mantra I shared, the body feels like there's nothing there, yes? Exactly. Now, if there's nothing there, how difficult is it to change it? How difficult is it to get healthy? How difficult is it to repair things? How difficult is it to overcome cancer? How difficult is it to transcend the concepts of life and death? If there's nothing there, how difficult is any of it?

The empowerment of knowing the truth that this body is just energy. I know it seems solid. I get it. But that illusion of limitation is caused by viewing the energy from the same frequential bandwidth that it vibrates within. In other words, from body consciousness. If you view the physical body from your Higher Mind, from a higher state of consciousness, you'll realize that it's pure energy and not physical.

Frequential Perspective

If you reduce yourself to body consciousness, you're viewing the physical form from the same low and limiting frequential bandwidth. You'll have the experience of physicality and solidity. If you don't view it from body consciousness, which is the awareness and wisdom that births these Self-mastery teachings, it allows one to transcend and transmute all so-called outer reality. Einstein said we can't solve a problem by viewing it from the same level of consciousness that created it. That is on the money.

It's the lower levels of consciousness that see problems due to its lack of holistic perspective and therefore limited understanding. It sees things as separate. The Higher Mind does not see nor create problems. There's simply creation, preservation, and destruction. Not problems.

There's nothing happening anywhere other than that cycle. The key is to create without the concept of limitation. Namely, without the limitations of the patterned subconscious egoic mind. It's the collapsing and contraction of consciousness, and therefore your energy.

Meditation Posture

A student asked, "RJ, how important do you feel meditation posture is?"

"That depends upon your level of expertise in terms of self-control and self-discipline," I replied. I have found that people who are not diligent meditators, proper posture helps exponentially. In general, for people who are not used to meditating effectively for more than five or ten minutes, proper posture increases their self-control and self-discipline. Proper posture aides in your dominion and command over your mind/body, which facilitates deep meditation.

Proper position promotes permanent precision. Once we become adept at meditating, it's perpetual with or without posture. Unbroken clarity. No finite mind and its delusions to overcome. That takes determination and devotion. In other words, it's either the pain of regret or the pain of self-discipline. Go with the latter.

But eventually posture or no posture, the one who meditates is gone. You (the I Am) is meditation. It's eternal and effortless. In the beginning, as one develops a self-inquiry and meditative practice, proper posture serves as a benefit multiplier.

Ideal Posture for Meditation

If you are seated, take note of the feeling of your back straight, feet placed firmly on the ground, palms up resting gently on the uppermost part of your thighs. Feel this. There's no tension. Tilt your head slightly downward so your soft gaze lands about six feet ahead on the floor. If the head is tilted slightly downward and your back is supported, you're no longer creating any resistance within your body.

Let your jaw be slightly open. No clenched mouth. Same with the tongue. We hold so much tension in our mouth all the time. The tongue is a muscle. With the mouth slightly open, let your tongue rest in the back in your mouth like a clam sitting in the back of its shell. I used to log in to people energetically when I first started teaching meditation, and the amount of tension held in the neck, jaw, and mouth was astounding.

You can feel how these proper instructions promote deeper states of meditation. If the body is holding any tension, it's going to require more of an effort to focus the mind. If you are uncomfortable, you'll be too preoccupied with body sensations. You don't want to be preoccupied with anything.

With proper posture, there is no tension. Pay close attention to your neck, mouth, and tongue. It's amazing how clenched we are in those areas. It's alarming. Do the proper posture all the time. Start incorporating it. Your meditation practice will flourish. Set yourself up for success.

The tension we hold in our back, neck, hands, mouth, and tongue is very debilitating and distracting. Start incorporating proper meditative posture and watch how much better you feel and how much more tangible your meditation is. You feel better in that posture even without the meditation.

The physical eyes will never see what it is I share with you. It's tangibly obvious to me, and that's why it's easy for me to explain and teach metaphysics. Tension and resistance happen when you identify with something, which is a contraction. The contraction of your energy from the collapsing of your consciousness is what creates tension and resistance.

Acceptance or agreement makes something real. And when you make something real, it becomes solid. That's what creates resistance. So does the denial of something. If you negate or rail against something, that makes it real as well. It too has become solid. That also creates resistance. Acceptance and denial create resistance.

Metaphysically, acceptance and denial do the exact same thing. They make it real. Now it's solid and resistance has been created. Allowance is the key. Allowance, my friends.

Detachment and Compassion

"Master RJ, there are people who function with emotional detachment and don't care, but they do not act aligned with love and compassion. So, the EMI feels tension around this. Can you help?" This question was asked during the many conversations we had during the five-month master class. Here's my reply:

Let's not misinterpret detachment for being a psychopath or sociopath. Having no empathy, right? It's the EMI's misinterpretation of what detachment tangibly is. It conceptualizes it to mean no love or compassion. It's the opposite. Detachment means you cease to misidentify yourself with anything. Now, you're fully present. Through detachment, what will flow from you is love and compassion, because the I Am is exactly that.

When the Light of Self-Realization Is Obscured

The EMI, when it doesn't care about anything or anyone, develops sociopathic and psychopathic tendencies. Clearly that's not what I'm talking about. This is narcissism. Not only do they not care, but they also have no empathy. Remember, caring is having a vested interest in a specific outcome. That is disempowering because it takes you out of now, which is where all your love, wisdom, and power reside. You want to be fully present. All of you here now, and what flows is compassion. And that's what love is. Narcissism is really the opposite of Self-realization. It's the other side of the coin.

Devote yourself and give yourself over to the teachings of Self-mastery. Take the ego mind, put it down, leave it alone, and never pick it back up again. All your troubles, all your concerns, anxiety, ruminations, projections, all of that belongs to the EMI. It does not serve. If you think that you need your EMI so your life doesn't fall apart, you're gravely mistaken. That life is not your life. It belongs to the matrix. You simply let yourself be recruited.

You operate with true joy, great efficiency, and tremendous power when your limitation program is not involved in your life. It diminishes everything and everyone, starting with yourself.

Timeless Truth 11

We move—not time—by the choices we make,
and this "movement" is either the evolution
or regression of consciousness.

What we experience as physical movement is, in actuality, a shift in perception. The I Am is endlessly experiencing the infinite facets of itself. It is either expanding its self-awareness or contracting its tangible understanding of itself. What we call movement is simply the shadow of illusion our light casts as it shifts in inner perception.

In the no-mind pure state of consciousness, there is no tangible recognition of the actor performing actions or physical movement. That is because both the actor and its actions are an illusion. They are simply a play within the outer screen of your consciousness. This outer play of actor and movement is always directed at the behest of the I Am-ness.

The I Am, while exploring its own limitless depth, projects a so-called person who performs actions to see itself in the act of experiencing, learning, and evolving itself. In the one true reality that eternally exists well beyond the five physical senses and the intellect, there is no outer world, no person, no actions, no movement. Simply, I Am.

EXERCISE
Actor or Actions

Look at every action your actor has ever performed. Are you that human actor and its actions or are you the awareness of that actor and its actions? If you are neither actor nor actions, how do they arise within your consciousness? What is actually—tangibly—occurring?

Has either actor or actions ever touched the I Am? Look deeply at this and journal your new understanding of actor, movement, and actions.

How We Can Create a Better World

A student asked, "Can we create a tangible different world with our I Am and Higher Mind?"

My reply, "Only with them."

"With our imagination and not thinking?" asked the student.

The currency of humanity is the EMI, which is a limitation program that runs by thinking. This is due to body consciousness (identification with form) that limits us to our low-frequency environment and cuts us off from our Higher Mind. Thinking is just the movement of the past based upon what is already here. We must align ourselves with our Higher Mind and our thinking will be driven by our limitless imagination rather than the attachments born of low-frequency body consciousness.

We must align ourselves directly with our inspiration, our highest desire. We then attach our intention to that inspiration born of the Higher Mind, and that information then trickles down one step, frequentially, into the lower astral, and then into the mental body. That process translates into only thinking about and subsequently manifesting your highest desire: your true inspiration.

The EMI is our summation of misperceptions, misunderstandings, and misidentifications. The Self is none of these things that we think or feel that we are. Now you can only think in terms of what you have already identified yourself with: beliefs, concepts, roles, ideologies, so-called knowledge, the body, or some experience. None of that is you. Listen to me carefully. None of that is you. You are the creator and awareness of it all. Just as the painter is not the painting, absolutely none of those things are you.

It's all the things and only the things you've bought into and misidentified yourself with that you can think about. You think about the concept of success you bought into and if you are good enough. You think about the religion you bought into and if you are pious enough. You think about the role you identify with and if you are living up to your concept of it. You think about this, and you think about that. You're thinking about what you heard the doctor say to you. What your mom and dad drilled into you. None of that is you. Which is why your character isn't you. That is why the EMI is so pathetic. The EMI is weak and ineffectual because it's completely and utterly inauthentic. It has no real power. Because it's not you!

The Highest Use of Creation

The goal is to infuse our lower astral and mental body with our true inspiration and highest desire born directly of the immeasurable I Am. Once aligned with the I Am, the astral, mental, emotional, etheric, along with the physical vehicle, all will be purified and electrically charged. This inner transcendence and direct alignment with the I Am will lead to the next enlightened society on Earth. This is the new age.

A master only thinks about what it intends to manifest. They have supreme self-control and self-discipline. Masters are the fulfillment and embodiment of certain aspects of the totality of what is. They reflect back to you your own divinity and perfection. That you are whole and complete as you are. Operate—create—from that knowingness. From the whole and complete Self. When you do that, everything that you give birth to will be whole and complete as well. The creation will lack nothing. Meaning it will serve your highest good and the highest good of all simultaneously.

When operating from and as the EMI, everything you create will be lacking, incomplete, and riddled with imperfections. The EMI is just a mimic, an actor performing actions. That actor is playing you! It's a low-frequency limitation program that runs by thinking. What's it going to create? Wholeness and completeness? Never. It's impossible.

We must create from our highest desire born of the Higher Mind. The order of creation is desire, intention, thought, emotion, action, and behavior. Align yourself to your highest desire and harness your intention. Unify Self, desire, and intention in the resting state. Once you do that through these teachings, the only thing you can ever think about and act upon is your highest desire. As I said, a master only thinks about what it intends to manifest. It is paramount to tangibly understand and embody this truth.

Chapter 13
Desire to Stillness

Practice non-engagement with the egoic mind and non-identification with the physical body, and true divinity will reveal itself.

It is the amount of attention and authenticity in your identifications to the programmed desires of finite mind and sensations of your physical body that give it such power. Underneath it all resides eternal divinity, timeless perfection, and unbreakable stillness.

Desire born of personhood only increases the disharmonious experience and weight of personhood. The more you desire and strive at the behest of your EMI, the more real and all-consuming your EMI becomes. Tracing the core motivation that fuels your desires (not acting upon them) is the only way to know your Self.

Only the desire to know Source/God/Creator will ever free you from earthly desire. Source/God/Creator is within your consciousness not outside of it. Set your desire and intention to know that which created and lives within you, and in everyone else, and all other desireless will cease.

MEDITATION
Turn Desire into Stillness

Close your eyes, take a deep breath in through the nose and exhale out the mouth. Repeat this three times.

Imagine that your mind/body complex is a biological spacesuit. You are simply wearing this spacesuit. You have no name, image, or form. Imagine that every thought is just the action of sentience sending energy into the mental body. What results are thoughts based upon identifications you mistakenly made during this trip to Earth.

Now imagine sending no energy anywhere through total and complete rest through gentle concentration. All your energy sits between your belly button and groin. All your sentience sits between your heart and spine. Give yourself permission to just be here now. Nothing but pure presence and unsullied awareness.

Imagine what it feels like to sink so far back into yourself that the mind/body complex requires no effort to engage it. You have no need to engage the biological suit because they run on their own without you. You are inside, protected, perfect, whole, and complete without them.

This is how to turn desire into stillness.

Protected, Perfect, Whole, and Complete

You have no need to engage the mind/body because it runs on its own. Because it's not you. You don't have to do anything to make your heart beat, your lungs breathe, your eyes see, your ears hear, and your nose smell. You don't have to do anything. Because it's not you. It's a biological vehicle. You are temporarily housed within it, protected, perfect, whole, and complete. Just let the body do what it was built to do and use no energy. Even as I move my hands and speak, I Am eternal stillness itself. This is how to turn desire to stillness.

A student asked, "Master RJ, may I share the impact this course has had on my life? I really am basically speechless about the effect this process that you are facilitating has had in my life. I mean, it's incredible. I was diagnosed in the midsummer with diabetes type 2. My blood sugar had gone from the high end of prediabetes just over the goal post and jumped a point and a half. So, a process of discipline that used the work and the meditation as the energy to have that 'discipline,' which really didn't take all that much effort. It just was so automatic. Long story short, in less than two and a half months, my blood sugar dropped two full points to normal.

"I mean, I'm a little ticked at my doctors because they haven't given me a gold star. Another one of the things that's happened along with this is it looks like I have a heart condition, whatever that might be. And they're trying to, well, it is all scheduled to go in for maybe stents. But I'm using this same energy. So, I wanted to pick up on how you can be just freed of, in my case, fear and anxiety. Which has kind of lightened up over the years, but it can still be there. Just this past Wednesday, I was having a little physical therapy and suddenly, the PT has me on the floor because basically I'm going unconscious.

"After the other doc sends me off to urgent care because I had fainted, they want to put me in a wheelchair. Anyway, during this whole experience, I was not freaking out. I'm just observing it. I'm not reading into it.

"I was experiencing it, and I was not upset. That, for me, is a miracle. It was just, well, they recommend this. I guess they kind of know what they're talking about. I'll just ride with it. Which by the way, I do not take to authority. I love your teachings, RJ. That's all I can say. Because I'm the one doing the work. It's total empowerment. This is a guru-free deal. You're just a delightful facilitator of metaphysics and higher truth. Thanks for bringing it through to this world. Thanks so much."

"Thank you very much," I said. "Congratulations on the work of bringing down the A1C." Imagine if millions of people knew the teachings of Self-mastery? To be able to heal without drugs and their lethal side effects. And without crazy effort either. All of us are already whole and complete as we are. The effort is performed by the actor, the EMI. When you reside within the fullness and completeness of the mighty I Am through these very simple yet liberating meditations, everything takes care of itself.

It's Always About the Self

It's not how hard you row, it's the boat that you're in. It's an effortless effort. It really is. These authentic Self-mastery teachings are prescriptive. I'm not doing anything. It's you.

You're doing it. I get asked it all the time, "How do you do these things, RJ?" I don't "do" anything. You guys do it. All of you are already "it." Eternally. Live that way, act that way, speak that way, love that way, forgive that way, create that way.

There are no limitations. There are no locks or bolts to anything. I don't care what it is. All limitations are self-imposed. The I Am is limitless. It is Source/God/Creator in action. Every time I'm here, I seemingly do the impossible, over and over. You know why? Because nothing is impossible. The best part of this course is you guys. I feel like I get in the way.

Each one of you is the master. I just make you remember. When you connect with me and hear me, you're seeing your own Self-realization and Self-mastery reflected back.

Desire and Intention

During the Self-mastery course, we discussed this question on desire and intention. A student asked, "Master RJ, my EMI has a question. Is desire to know or achieve different from the desire and intention that is considered to have the highest frequency?"

Yes. We are speaking about the desires born of personhood as opposed to the desire to tangibly know Source/God/Creator. They don't have anything in common with one other. The desires of the EMI (of personhood) are all the transitory phenomena you've aligned yourself with since you arrived here. They don't have anything to do with the I Am or God directly, which are the same thing.

The beliefs, concepts, body identification, ideologies, so-called knowledge—the currency of fetid perversions and ignorance that passes for world culture—these are illusions and delusions that make up your EMI. Those are the desires of personhood. You are not a person, you are an immortal, perfect, divine fractal of God having a fleeting physical experience. Period.

Do you wish to transcend all these earthly desires born of personhood right now? Let's return to my childhood mantra. Close your eyes. Using the silent inner spoken word, repeat after me, "The body is nothing. The body is nothing. The body is nothing. The body is nothing. The body is nothing. The body is nothing. The body is nothing."

Do you sincerely want to transcend all mind/body limitations and the desires born of it? Perform that mantra with sincere devotion and fervent desire. Perform it like your life depends upon your liberation! Watch what happens.

The authentic mystics and masters are really escape artists. It's not Houdini. They have escaped the tyranny of the finite mind and limiting body consciousness. They are the greatest escape artists of all time.

The authentic teachings of Self-mastery allow you to experience these things and move right through and beyond them without becoming addicted or attached here. That's really the key: Detachment. As Christ said, "Be in the physical but not of the physical." Allow the mighty I Am to drive the bus of what is co-created here.

When the I Am is operating there is no lower consciousness interference and delusion. That delusion creates the reality and the solidity of duality: right and wrong, good and bad. It's all judgment born of separation, fragmentation, and compartmentalization. Lies. They're illusions. It's all one thing. Existence is one thing. Shall I give my silly analogy about peanut butter cookies again?

Peanut Butter Cookie Dough and the Collective Consciousness

Let's revisit our peanut butter cookie dough analogy. My partner and I love to make peanut butter cookies. You make the dough, add the peanut butter, the nuts, the chocolate, coconut shavings. I'm getting hungry just talking about it. You have this big bowl of cookie dough.

You then take out the cookie sheet and start making dollops of the dough and place them onto the cookie sheet. Now, no matter how hard you try, you can't make the dollops of cookie dough uniform.

It's just impossible. They're never quite the same size. Some have a little more peanut butter, more chocolate, more nuts, or coconut shavings. It doesn't matter how much time you take, there's going to be variance. Now you're starting to understand God's intention. Evolution through variance.

You place all the individual balls of cookie dough onto the sheet, and they're all different. Now imagine that the little balls of cookie dough start to become self-aware. Does this sound familiar? Through their self-awareness, they begin to compare. "Hey, wait a minute. Why are you bigger than me? Why do you have more peanut butter? How come I don't have as much coconut shavings as you do?"

Through their temporarily individualized but severely limited self-awareness, there's immediate comparison and shortly thereafter lack, jealousy, and competition. But one second ago, they were all one. Same with us.

Labels Tear Apart What Is Eternally Whole

Once you label something good, you create the concept of bad. Once you label something beautiful, you create the concept of ugly. This is duality. The more you believe in the authenticity of your labels, the more these things become real. The more you will suffer and engender suffering.

These teachings (the wisdom that transcends knowledge) is your get-out-of-jail-free card. You become Houdini. You escape the tyranny of the egoic mind and limiting body consciousness. This is freedom. Your mere presence here will serve as a lighthouse for all those lost in the dark. You become a teacher of the new earth.

Using the silent inner spoken word. Say it with me, "May every notion I give birth to bring about the victory of light."

Timeless Truth 12

Source/God/Creator is the summation of all wisdom—unconditional love—and expresses itself by endowing humanity with the free will to experience whatever it most desires, always on its return journey from nowhere to where we eternally remain: the Oneness of unconditional love.

We ultimately go nowhere as we eternally remain inside and part of Source/God/Creator. There is only here and now. Consciousness simply creates challenges and obstacles so it can see itself in the act of overcoming them. This is the only real evolution: the accrual of sentience. You and your life plan are just that. It is a microcosm of the macrocosm.

Your Higher Self creates you so it can evolve through and as you. Your Higher Self was created by Source/God/Creator so it can evolve and learn about itself concurrently. Its core, the very wellspring of being and non-being, is the vibration of love. The further we get away from the essence of ourselves, the further we get away from the only truth: love.

The only death and discord we ever experience is the love we withhold from ourselves, and therefore each other. Give yourself what you most fervently desire: your own love. Surrender and let your heart explode *now* and it shall dissolve all that cannot endure such perfection, majesty, and divinity. God is waiting, patiently, and only yearns for your love.

EXERCISE
Pure Love

What does love actually feel like? What are its tangible qualities? Journal and explore this. Love precedes all mental concepts and bodily sensations. Search your heart deeply. Open your heart and make your mind realize its Master. Just for today, only act in complete accordance with this love. With every notion you give birth to let it be an act of pure love. Let it envelop your entire being. Journal this and never betray yourself—your love—again.

Journal what this realization gives you.

Life Is a Blank Canvas

No thought, in and of itself, has any weight. All thoughts are equal in weightlessness. All of them. It is your belief in the authenticity of the thought, and your subsequent identification to it, that gives it gravitas and sway over your consciousness and subsequently your body of energy.

Life itself is a blank canvas for the immortal creator within us all to create. Nothing has any inherent meaning. And it doesn't mean anything that it doesn't mean anything. Now, what meaning are you going to ascribe to that?

Enlightenment and even Self-mastery is the effortless unending flow upon the river of compassion and joy. The truth of how things really are is far more loving and kinder than your mind can ever fathom.

I know the EMI has conceptualized what these states of being and states of consciousness are like, because that's how limited the EMI is. I promise you that the truth is that it's filled with joy, laughter, and lightness. It's only the egoic mind that takes itself seriously and therefore turns the play of life into a tragedy. I joke around all the time. I have trouble being "serious." We didn't invent humor, but we can certainly avail ourselves of it endlessly. Light-heartedness births the joy of transcendent creativity.

Without further haste, I shall present my case.
The name of the game, without any claim to fame,
is to not blame or shame.
What you feign, by any name,
shall wane because all pain is in vain.
Don't complain, just refrain,
and the stain of disdain shall no longer remain!

Hard as the 'I' may try to procrastinate or satiate;
it must create for all heaven's sake!

Okay, I'll stop with the lyrical bits. Whatever it is that you are passionate about and excited about, that puts you in the flow state. Do that. Doesn't matter what it is. Who cares. Anything that puts you in direct communion and unification with your highest excitement. When you're doing that, what you're experiencing is yourself—the Higher Self—directly. Notice how this is not mental machinations or physical gratification. You are enjoying the Self. You are enjoying yourself. Think about those words. The Self is the flow state.

During the Self-mastery class, a student commented, "Funny how school programming is all memorizations. The opposite of spontaneity."

Yes. How funny, isn't it? Let what comes, come. Let what goes, go. What remains? You. Instead of lamenting on what you do not have, realize what it is that you have never lost.

Life and death are concepts. Consciousness and energy are eternal. Let what comes, come. Let what goes, go. What remains? You. Untouched by it all. Untouched, unscathed, unsullied, unbreakable. That's you.

The concept you hold of yourself is merely a single viewpoint within a sea of endless viewpoints. Therefore, it is a singular momentary contraction, a limitation and only matters to the identifier of the single viewpoint: the temporary human character. Alter your viewpoint, your perception, by expanding your inner understanding and everything changes even though nothing has changed. You can change one thousand times in a single day and still be wearing the same clothes.

The I Am creator creates and everything changes because you are everything. The Immortal Self, I Am, does not require self-confining parameters such as mental concepts or a physical vehicle. Your human character, the EMI, is downstream from the I Am and therefore clings to the temporary because it too is temporary.

The Inner Shift That Creates Reality

I want you to shift into allowance. Not acceptance, *allowance*. Feel the difference when you say those words. Feel what happens to you. This is real metaphysics, my friends. As I say the word *acceptance*, I'm collapsing the word together over the stomach with my hands. Acceptance is a contraction. You can feel it. You can feel it collapse beneath your heart chakra and above your belly. Feel the energy collapse when you say acceptance.

Now say allowance. *Allowance*. Feel the expansion. Feel the night and day difference between those two words. It's immediate and it's tangible. That's real metaphysics, real eternal truth. So now simply expand and shift into allowance. Allow that moment that was traumatic, I don't care what it was, shift and allow that moment to simply be just one way. The infinite possible possibilities, the infinite spaciousness within you, can reveal and express themselves to you.

Allowance Rewrites the Past and Creates the Future

Allowance gives you the power to shift out of a fixed reality and into the infinite spaciousness of the Immortal Self. You are allowing yourself to experience a past event with a completely different perception and understanding. You are literally changing your past—now—and creating a whole new future—now. That is because there really is no past. If the past was fixed, we wouldn't be able to do this, would we?

Just underneath acceptance is agreement. If you are in acceptance, you are agreeing that this is the one and only reality, and therefore it becomes fixed. Allowance is the opposite. Allowance opens you up to all the infinite possible possibilities within yourself and therefore how you can perceive and understand any moment. And all things can now manifest within the screen of your consciousness because you are in a state of allowance. It is allowance that lowers the drawbridge for you to receive true abundance in every way.

To receive, you must be in a state of allowance. If you are in acceptance or agreement (and I realize acceptance is a spiritual buzzword) but it is complete unawakened nonsense, it locks you into one perceived and most often a discordant and disharmonious reality. And you're told "that's just the way it is. You have to accept it." You then further spell yourself by repeating "I've been traumatized." That's my story, that's my identity, and I'm sticking to it. I have all these things wrong with me because I was traumatized. Now, I am justified and have solidified my disharmony.

"I'm justified in having all these things wrong with me, RJ, because it was traumatic." None of you want to operate that way. You don't have to. No one must. It's the shift from acceptance into allowance. Go back to any events that were difficult for you. Simply allow that to be just one way that it manifested itself (one way, not the way) and start to see it from a different perspective.

Allow yourself to see and feel the infinite possible possibilities within as it pertains to how you can now perceive yourself and therefore understand that event. Give yourself the permission to see it completely differently. Rewrite your past now by shifting from acceptance into allowance.

Self-Mastery Is Anti-Personal Development

Truth is not meant to be memorized. I don't want your human character memorizing these teachings and then regurgitating it. That is useless. We don't really learn anything that way. We learn about ourselves by experiencing ourselves tangibly. The truth is tangible. It's immediate, simple, and powerful. Memorization is only sought after and a characteristic of the unawakened mind.

Personal development is memorization. I am not here to increase your personhood. The goal is not to develop personhood. Liberation is not personal development. Tangibly expand your self-awareness, and therefore the blossoming of authentic Self-realization, not your human character. Don't create a bigger illusion, a bigger identity, a bigger story. Do the opposite. Wake up in the dream. Fully waking up is God Consciousness. We are setting the table for the feast of eternal wisdom with the tenets of Self-mastery and Timeless Truths.

Flow with the meditations that accompany them all day, every day. Embody them, my friends.

Incarnation and the Creation of Our Life Plan

The human experience is simply an accelerant for the evolution of consciousness. Incarnation is a way to evolve, and when we do it properly, we evolve our consciousness—which is deepening of our eternal reservoir of love and wisdom—with the greatest efficacy. Source/God/Creator is obsessed with evolving itself with the greatest efficacy, and I am of the exact same mind.

Let's look more deeply at what happens through incarnation into the lower frequencies. We reduce ourselves to body consciousness so the whole experience becomes greatly limiting and incredibly challenging. And through the limitations and challenges we experience: we learn and evolve.

Only through that severest of limitations and monumental challenges can we experience the specific things that are only available to us here in the lower frequencies. In higher frequencies, in more holistic environments and states of consciousness, the challenges are not very challenging. Does that make sense?

Do we put all these challenges and obstacles into our life plan? Absolutely. Before we incarnate, there is an extensive list of data points we create. For now, I am going to reduce it to four main things so we can get a "flavah" of the things that we decide upon prior to any incarnation.

The first one we choose is the form factor. Meaning human or alien. Those are our only two choices for incarnation. Once sentience has evolved to a certain level, it would not incarnate into a plant, an insect, or an animal form because that does not match up with the level of sentience that would be operating that physical vehicle. All of us had the choice of human vehicle or alien vehicle prior to this incarnation.

The second we choose is the frequency that we want to incarnate into. I know everyone says we're in the third dimension going into 5D (totally wrong from my perspective—we're in the third frequency). We could have chosen the fourth, the fifth, the sixth, the seventh, the eighth, the ninth, the tenth. Once you get to the eleventh, you can still incarnate into that, but it's almost like not an incarnation. Earth is a pan-frequential being. It exists in all those frequencies simultaneously and there are realities with human civilizations on all of them.

We also choose the timeline. Remember, when you are outside of space-time, it is almost like you are looking at it like when Neo from the *Matrix* meets the Architect. I think that was the second film called *Matrix Reloaded*. Imagine you are in a room with fifty television sets all set up and each one is a different timeline. There is the fourth century, there is the twenty-sixth century, there is the eighth century, there is the thirty-eighth century, there is 2000 BC, et cetera, et cetera. You insert yourself into the movie timeline of your choice, literally.

We also choose what team we are going to play for. The goodies or the baddies. Team light or team dark. We choose it all. And I promise you, everyone here, everyone in the incarnation cycle, has played both good guy and bad guy endlessly. There are many more experiences within the life plan, but those hopefully remove a lot of mystery and spiritual fiction.

Law of Cause and Effect

Remember what I said about giving birth to any notion. You must know it inside out, top to bottom, backward and forward. Everyone plays the bad guy, and everyone plays the good guy over and over. That way we understand everything that we ever give birth to. It is all part of evolving as an immortal creator. We must see it and experience in every possible way.

Are there even powerful souls or more evolved souls that will play the bad guy? Yes, of course. Most of the time they are behind the scenes, but not all the time. Often, we don't get to see them, but they are pulling the strings. There are many black magicians incarnate right now. I'm not going to name them. It's just a role in a movie.

A student asked me, "Why create a human incarnation to know human experiences? Source/God/Creator already knows all there is to know."

Let's shatter some illusions right now. Source/God/Creator is not all-knowing. For anyone who can authentically commune directly with Source/God/Creator, you know exactly what I'm talking about. It is an unfathomable intelligence. It is a wisdom and a love that is so far beyond human comprehension, that it would certainly seem that Source/God/Creator is all-knowing. But Source/God/Creator is not all-knowing. Source/God/Creator creates to fully understand itself and its infinite potential. It is really important to understand that.

From a human perspective, Source/God/Creator is all-knowing. That perspective is mostly from religious dogma, which is the energy you've aligned with that is driving your question. I said we were going to shatter some illusions. Source/God/Creator is creating to understand itself. Just as you are creating to understand yourself.

Existence is perpetually evolving. The human experience is for Source/God/Creator to understand the minutia of itself. You can think of us, a human being, as an atom of Source/God/Creator. So, for Source/God/Creator to understand its own minutia, it needed to create something that could understand itself at that level.

It's just a belief, and beliefs have nothing to do with what is. It's just a story that you have limited your understanding to.

When I was a kid, I would project my consciousness, so I was tiny enough to walk between the blades of grass. The grass was tall as trees. I wanted to understand the minutia of my backyard. I was playing, creating, and exploring. Source/God/Creator has created tiny, tiny aspects of itself: us.

God wants to even experience limitations or the temporary experience of a limitation. There are no tangible or authentic limitations, but there is the experience of a limitation. And with that in mind, it created the lower frequencies of the physical universe where we are cut off from the greater reality. Therefore, there is an inherent limitation built in because we reduce ourselves to body consciousness, the functionality of the human suit. Think about what we can learn when you are completely cut off from the Higher Self and the greater reality. That's what is going on.

In that sense, it is a limitation, until you realize there are no limitations. Self-mastery is when you are completely detached from name, image, and form, and you realize there are no limitations. You can still explore everything, experience everything, but not through body consciousness. So, it is to experience the limitation because there is something to learn by experiencing the lower frequencies. In comparison to the greater reality, it is a limitation. Does that make sense?

Question about Karma

A student asked the following: "RJ, if we are playing both good and bad people in the incarnations, whenever we play the bad person, will we not continue to create karma?"

First, let's talk about karma. Most hear about karma as "What goes around, comes around." Or, "Karma's a b#%*#!" However, this idea of karma as it's been co-opted by Western cultures, isn't accurate. Buddhist and Hindu traditions don't describe karma as something to be created or accumulated. Instead it's an awareness of how the energy we have—the actions we do—relate to our lives, past, present, and future. As I tangibly understand it and can see it clearly, *karma* isn't the accurate word to use. Instead, we're thinking more of negative energy or low frequencies and how those drive addiction or attachment to anything here on Earth.

When we become addicted or attached to anything, it is our energy that we are using to become attached. Like Spider-Man shooting his spider web, our energy is the spider web. Once we are addicted or attached, we are energetically stuck. We are going nowhere. It stops our evolutionary progression. We can only undue our attachment in the location of where we are energetically stuck.

There is a soul that exists (that is, of course, part of its Higher Self) that has developed the skills and ability to be the "bad guy," and it does it very well. Exceedingly well. Now, from a higher-consciousness perspective, by being the worst possible person, this soul can engender a global wave of compassion that blankets the earth. By knowingly doing the worst, most heinous things possible this soul's life plan is to be such a bad guy that everyone realizes that we don't ever want this experience again.

Really listen to what I am saying because how things really work is the opposite of the human intellect. Think of the bravery and courage it takes to play that role. This soul will receive and endure the endless hatred emanated from humanity toward it. And this soul keeps volunteering to do this. Are you that brave? This soul is incredibly courageous. It still hasn't recovered from its last incarnation. We owe it a huge debt of gratitude and our respect.

Now, when we look at this from the limited human perspective, we like to say that we should have killed that person. Even as a child before it could do these things. The souls that sign up to play the "victims" of the carnage do so willingly and with full knowledge. Why? So, you don't have to. It's how they can be of service. The real truth about atrocity is to engender compassion. And then, forgiveness. There is an entire multiverse of understanding that our little intellect can never understand.

All the World's a Stage

Think of a play. You go to the theater. There's the protagonist and antagonist. They are at each other's throats the whole play, right? Very entertaining. It seems so real. And that is the point. They must really hate each other, right? Then the curtain comes down and they are immediately hugging and high fiving each. All the actors are effusive about what a great performance. Then they go have a beer together after the play. It is a little bit like that.

With this understanding, how does one ever stop this low-frequency energy loop? With nonidentification and non-attachment.

Detachment severs all energetic chords. Negative energy is addiction to anything here. It has nothing to do with what role we play.

The concepts of good and bad are irrelevant. They don't authentically or intrinsically exist. We could do horrible things because we choose to play the bad character for evolutionary purposes, but we would not create karma if we don't get attached to anything.

Same with playing the good guy. Don't get attached to playing the role of being pious or being so saintly. It's still a character and if you get attached to the feeling of being better than everyone, of being spiritually superior, you are creating karma.

We shattered many illusions today. Authentic liberation—true Self-mastery—has nothing to do with any label, identity, or role. What we all are is light years beyond anything we could even imagine. I Am that I Am.

Conclusion

My twenty-week Self-mastery course, like all my live courses, is unlike anything taught on this planet, or any planet for that matter. The profound impact and transformation that people experience is literally life changing and extraordinary. It speaks to depth of power and timeless truth contained within the teachings. The quality of people's moment-to-moment existence is forever raised in frequency and their consciousness eternally expanded.

The feedback I have received since I first taught this course in 2022 has been so overwhelming that I carved out a five-month block of time in 2023 to teach it once more. The joy, connectivity, and liberation my students experience is beyond moving. Because of this, I am proud to say, I will be teaching it a third time in 2024 as well. It's worth noting, I never intended to teach this course more than once.

What I find just as interesting as the life-altering effect these teachings have on my students, is the shift that occurs in me as well. This shift is not the same that my students experience who are encountering these timeless teachings for the first time. For me, there is a deep sense of gratitude, honor, and an incomprehensibly awesome responsibility I feel. It literally speaks to the very core of my existence and is a tangible reminder of exactly why I am here now.

The joy and communion that is experienced by both my students and myself through participation in these teachings is unlike anything else. For all of us to tangibly experience the depth of what we are with such crystalline clarity is beyond measure. It is so humbling to see the freedom and liberation in my students that I too lose myself in the timelessness of our connectivity and communion. The unconditional love that is felt among us all is a treasure well worth the agony and suffering we have all experienced throughout our lifetimes.

When a student shares with me that through these teachings that they have overcome years, decades, even an entire lifetime of suffering, there are no words to express how I feel. I have often wept tears of joy right along with them. To tangibly see and hear expressed that these teachings have saved their life is beyond humbling. It removes personhood from the entire experience and brings all of us closer to the truth, that we are all one.

Teaching this course has changed me in terms of the role I play with humanity. I learn every day from the incredible souls who take my courses. Their incredible insights, fresh perspectives, and open-mindedness affords me the opportunity to stretch as a teacher. To be able to go deeper and deeper into the realms far beyond the finite mind. I have learned how to better communicate the indescribable nor understandable in ways that hit home for everyone because of my expansive and diverse students. I am a better teacher because of them and therefore a greater servant.

I can recall a few decades ago, I was told by Source/God/Creator that if I help just one person, my mission here on Earth will have been a success. I have never forgotten that. That message is within every beat of my heart. I now see success as if I can help one person every day, every hour, every minute, and every second through all my teachings, books, interviews, videos, and courses that my presence here on Earth will have raised the frequency of humanity and this planet in ways not yet tangibly realized or even barely understood.

Like all my work, the Self-mastery course is deeply personal. When I say personal, I do not mean personhood. I am speaking about revealing and being my True Self. My courses allow me to fully be me. There is nothing more joyous, fulfilling, meaningful, purposeful, loving, and powerful than embodying who and what you really are. Every time I work with people, I experience this gift of the I Am presence and like all gifts, they are best when shared. This course has changed me. It further deepens and anchors my mind/body complex to the truth of what I Am. It sharpens my ability as a servant. It hones my skills of manifestation. It expands and unfurls my talents as a healer. Most importantly, it reminds me of why I ever incarnate anywhere within the multiverse. It is the love I feel in my heart that brings me back. And this love transforms all who come in contact with it.

The New You, the New Earth

Working with the teachings of this book (and all my books), their power and efficacy is immediate and tangible. The inner shift into greater self-awareness, self-expression, and a superior quality of life is the evolution of consciousness. Because we are conditioned to deify the intellect (for the nefarious reasons outlined in this book), we associate humanity's awakening with technological advancements. Never forget, the greatest technology was, is, and forever shall be your consciousness.

The new earth may very well have incredible technological advancements that make our current technologies seem barbaric. Things like time travel, remedies for disease, and free energy were discovered long ago, my friends. They have been kept secret and hidden. Part of our inner shift as we ascend the frequencies may very well include the slow dissemination and availability of these technologies.

The new you is the one who can and will use great power for the betterment of all. The new earth nor the new you has yet to make itself tangibly known and permanent because the addictions and identification with body consciousness and therefore materialism have yet to be transcended. As we awaken to who and what we really are, the new you and the new earth will go hand in hand. The enlightened teachings of Self-mastery will usher in a new consciousness that this planet has not seen in tens of thousands of years.

What can one expect as the new you emerges from the shadows of misperception, misunderstanding, and misidentification? What does one experience as the Self is liberated from nonstop societal conditioning, brainwashing, and trauma-based mind control that we call world culture? *Freedom!* The clarity, courage, and power of the mighty I Am shall return this world, and you, to its original and eternal state: perfection and paradise.

The new you will always precede the new earth. One cannot wait for the mirror to smile first. As we attune ourselves to the wisdom that transcends knowledge, the so-called outer world will reflect our inner luminosity and geometrical congruence. It is our vibration, and the higher our frequency is the more our true vibration emanates unabated, that gives rise to all shape and form. Think of it this way, the material world is like undifferentiated stem cells, ready to become whatever it is programmed to be through desire and intention.

The new you will not be a programmed drone that mindlessly obeys whatever net of inversion and perversion currently is being cast. These mind programs are distilled by fetid institutions corrupted by those who despise your eternal purity and kind nature. All the world's a stage and the new you will not be fooled by the gesticulations and obfuscations of bad actors paraded before us.

The new you will possess razor clarity and therefore be unscathed, unharmed, and shall laugh at the endless and impotent charade. The background music of nails screeching along a chalkboard will no longer send shivers down your spine. Rather, you shall stand tall, resolute in the knowingness that all this was always for your growth. To make your back stronger and your heart more tender. And you will know, all trials and tribulations were designed by you for your own evolution. In this moment it will be obvious, and you will know more deeply and tangibly than anything you have ever known or felt: that you are the mighty and in full stature now!

Say that command, my friend: "I am the mighty; I am in full stature, now!" Feel every word. Let the purple flame of transmutation consume all that is not germane to you. Say it again: "I am the mighty;

I am in full stature, now!" That is the light of the new you and the new earth shall reflect your multifaceted brilliance, luminescence, and victory over darkness.

How to Move Forward

The best way to move forward is to simply pretend you just arrived here, no past, no future. This brings the unconditioned I Am forth. Now the Real You is present. Your being-ness is now online and simply put your being-ness into your doing-ness. This is how to always be your best and to create a life that only direct attunement with the I Am can manifest. Take notice at how simple this is, my friend. That is because you need nothing. You already are, always have been, and forever will be whole, complete, and perfect. You are a fractal of Source/God/Creator endlessly and eternally experiencing your limitless nature.

In order to move forward, we cannot be attached to anything or anyone, including your own incarnation. Removing your personal agenda born of personhood and detachment from everything you are does not happen automatically. In order to know yourself deeply and fully, one must let go of everything. Whatever you are holding on to isn't you. Instead of lamenting and struggling over what comes and goes, realize the one thing you have never lost: you. It is the immortal time lapse camera of all experience.

Moving forward requires no effort. The momentum you have accrued through these teachings shall carry across hurricane waters. Only by hanging on to the past and agonizing over the future do we create the experience of struggle. All of that suffering has nothing to do with now. Now contains everything. All of your love, wisdom, compassion, power, courage, talents, clarity, and forgiveness can only be tangibly accessed when you are fully present. If all of that, everything that you eternally are, is not good enough, then you have let your EMI rob you of everything.

Moving forward with courage, humility and grace is the way of the Masters. Because you have endured the slings and arrows of low-frequency existence, you have realized the highest truth: life in and of itself has no meaning. It is the gentle tenacity of self-control and self-discipline that awakens your indomitable will and limitless nature. Only then does the magic of the I Am presence reign supreme.

By tangibly being the limitless divine fractal of Source/God/Creator that we are, we imbue each moment with our love, wisdom, talents, and abilities for our highest good and the betterment of all simultaneously. They are no longer separate. Duality has been vanquished by the One Self within us all. There are no others. The way forward is to live this way, act this way, be this way, love this way, forgive this way, play this way, and create this way.

You do not need permission from anyone or anything to live your best life nor do you need permission to be the best version of yourself. The only thing that can ever stop an immortal, limitless, whole, and complete Creator is separation, duality. That is the patterned subconscious egoic mind. We can only stop ourselves by allowing the harsh inner critic inside our head, that has been programmed into us, to have dominion over our love and freedom. That voice inside your head is not you. It is an illusion. The emperor has no clothes.

The EMI is a limitation program that runs by thinking. It is the unholy trifecta of misperceptions, misunderstandings, and misidentifications. Tis nothing but a shadow cast by the towering light of the mighty I Am. The teachings in this book remove all blinders. The wisdom that transcends knowledge shall usher in a new way of being. You, my friend, are a teacher of this new Earth. You are what this world, and your world, cries out for. Unleash your Self. I am waiting for you to join me once again.

I remain your holy brother, in freedom.

RJ

Appendix 1
12 Tenets of Self-Mastery

Below are the twelve tenets of Self-mastery, their respective explanations and specific meditations that accompanies each of the teachings.

Tenet 1: Separateness to Oneness

When we devote ourselves to clarity, calmness, connectivity, and communion with the Oneself within, we walk with God.

Space-time creates the experience of separateness which births the concept of relationships. This temporary state of delusion leads to duality. When we limit our sentience to body consciousness, an illusory and transient subject/object paradigm encases, fragments, and compartmentalizes universal super consciousness. This contraction of consciousness prevents the tangible experience of our collective Higher Mind and eternal Oneness.

Through the cessation analysis, the dualistic nature of our fragmented lower consciousness ceases to exist. As the subject/object paradigm disintegrates, so does your experience of separation from Source/God/Creator and therefore all life. Duality no longer exists. The One who sees through your eyes sees through all eyes. It's all God. See and experience yourself and everyone this way now.

Do not seek to understand through a subject/object paradigm. This construct is the collapsing of consciousness, an illusion born of an unawakened mind. Instead, know the truth. Know thyself—the Oneself within us all. Only by the eternal silencing of your finite mind will the polyphonic symphony of existence be heard and tangibly known once again.

Separateness to Oneness is how we walk with God.

MEDITATION
Experience Separateness to Oneness

Close your eyes, take a deep breath in through the nose, and exhale out the mouth. Repeat this three times.

Pretend you just arrived here, no past, no future. Imagine what it would feel like to abandon all personal agendas. Let the purity of non-desire and its supreme vibration wash over you completely. Let it forever change your immortal state of being. Know that everyone, all existence, at its core is precisely this: agenda-less and free. Now, see all life with the eyes of purity.

Journal what this experience is like.

Tenet 2: Attachments to Freedom

Do what you know to be tangibly known to be true and expect no results.

Freedom is not doing whatever you want whenever you want. Freedom is escaping the tyranny of the finite mind and its limiting body consciousness. The lower consciousness or EMI is not free. It perpetually and fecklessly seeks to balance and harmonize its eternal and immutable incompleteness. Freedom is not possible for the subconscious patterned egoic mind. The EMI can only seek the satiation of its desires which in turn creates, justifies, reinforces, and perpetuates its own suffering.

Pleasure is trying to relive the past. Pain is trying to escape the future. Through non-thought, past and future disappear. The voice inside your head is the spell you put over your consciousness and therefore your body of energy. By not "spelling" yourself with past and future, you will cease to conjure up your own suffering. Through the normalization of non-thought, your attachments wither and die upon the vine of clarity, calmness, courage, and creativity. Your true nature—Freedom—will be tangibly known once again.

Whatever and whomever your energy is attached to is your master. You cease to have any self-control when attachments exist. Whatever you are attached to has control over you. Without self-control, there can be no freedom. Without freedom, your life lacks individual fulfillment. Without individual purpose and fulfillment, freedom has no meaning.

Releasing attachments and experiencing freedom gives life purpose and meaning.

MEDITATION
Experience Attachments to Freedom

Close your eyes, take a deep breath in through the nose, and exhale out the mouth. Repeat this three times.

Pretend your two eyes are not attached to your brain. Command all your energy to return to you. All cords and attachments are now severed. Imagine what it feels like to have all your energy back within your body. Feel the completeness of total freedom and the massive increase in energetic power.

Now, close your eyes. Imagine what it feels like to have no name, no image, no form. Just awareness and power. What does this feel like? All so-called physicality, thoughts, and emotions are mere shadows projected by this invisible, eternal, formless force. Everything is an illusion other than the imageless, nameless, formless force that is you.

Journal what this experience feels like.

Tenet 3: Disorder to Order

Cultivate inner stillness and silence as it reveals the intuitive wisdom to perceive and understand the one true reality.

The created constructs of past and future cloud the crystalline clarity of Christ consciousness. Once the machinations of the finite mind are believed in, attachment to the body follows. With identification to the physical form, we are reduced to limiting body consciousness. With the adoption and immersion into body consciousness, the physical world is born. Now, disorder will forever live within the chaos of your conditioned mind.

To remove disorder born of past and future, one must question the questioner. Your conditioned mind (personhood) is imprisoned within the concepts of time. Only in silence and patience does the flower of wisdom bloom. It is thought that creates the delusion of knowledge and the illusion of time. Meditation (the Self) annihilates the very concept that you are merely human.

Disorder is thought. It is nothing more than electromagnetic interference bathed in e-motion. This bathing creates identification and now the body is sufficiently charged to act. The actor who performs these actions is your EMI (ego/mind/identity). Only in silencing the electromagnetic interference will you realize that none of this endless charade is you.

MEDITATION
Move from Disorder to Order

Close your eyes, take a deep breath in through the nose, and exhale out the mouth. Repeat this three times.

Say to yourself: "I don't know, and I don't care." This empties both your mental and emotional containers. You can effortlessly maintain total mental clarity and perpetual emotional freedom because this is I Am-ness. There is no effort or straining to maintain I Am. Disorder turns to order only when you finally give yourself permanent permission to relax mentally and emotionally.

This is how to move from disorder to order.

Journal the difference between the qualities of disorder and order.

Tenet 4: Ignorance to Wisdom

Imagination through inspiration for the betterment of all is the highest use of the creative force.

The reason your mind wants more and more information is because it doesn't know anything. It is eternally bankrupt of self-knowledge. The mind forever and fecklessly attempts to balance its total ignorance with information. It does this out of fear to have something to cling to. Fear (ignorance of Self) is caused by identification with electromagnetic interference and can only germinate in the absence of the divine.

Wisdom flows on the river of intuition. Ignorance (fear) blocks the tangible recognition of your true vibration. This prevents the flow and integration of your Higher Mind (in the form of intuitive wisdom and limitless imagination) into the incarnation. Ignorance cannot be overcome with the intellect. They are both prisoners, enslaved within the confines of the conditioned mind.

Only by replacing ignorance (the fear-based habituation of thinking) with pure I Am (meditation) will ignorance die. What blooms in the silence and patience of self-awareness is wisdom. It will flow unabated when there is no electromagnetic interference blocking its signal. Alignment with your own Higher Mind turns ignorance into wisdom.

MEDITATION
Move from Ignorance to Wisdom

Close your eyes, take a deep breath in through the nose, and exhale out the mouth. Repeat this three times.

Ask yourself a question that you do not know the answer to, nor do you care what the answer is. This exercise engenders the "no mind no attachment state." Stay in this state of clarity and peace by granting yourself permission to not know or care about anything right now. Let all your mental and emotional energies dissipate.

Now, begin to realize that without believing in the weight or authenticity of any question or the questioner, knowing will flow through you without effort. Without trying to figure out through mentalization, allow your intuitive wisdom to speak, not with words but with knowingness.

This is how to go from ignorance to wisdom.

Tenet 5: Violence to Kindness

See yourself in all beings and know that there is no need to renounce, covet, or destroy.

Thought rips apart the fabric of what is eternally whole and complete, starting with yourself. Beliefs and concepts are simply a string of thoughts. With every thought you identify yourself with, you take yourself further and further out of alignment. Once you have committed to this violence unto yourself, you then do this to everyone and everything.

You must first deceive yourself to deceive others. You are first violent with yourself—in the form of beliefs, concepts, and ideologies—which then serve as the justification for violence inflicted upon others. All physical and emotional violence first begins as an idea in the thought realm. Self-talk is the quiet violence we inflict upon ourselves which always precedes and used as justification for the atrocities we commit upon so-called others.

There are no others. All forms of separation are violence. The lower conditioned mind cannot see nor understand what it is doing. Only by residing in and experiencing what exists prior to thought does one foment the ability to transmute violence into kindness.

MEDITATION
Transmute Violence into Kindness

Close your eyes, take a deep breath in through the nose, and exhale out the mouth. Repeat this three times.

Imagine that your head is simply a periscope, just pure perception sans analysis. The captain (you) who looks through the periscope is way down deep in the hull of the ship, between your heart and spine. Experience yourself and the projected outside world through this analogy. Resist the habituation of your conditioned mind to analyze and judge anything you perceive.

As you marinate within and as this awareness, allow your sense of self to extend outward to everything you perceive. What you perceive is simply an outward projection that comes from within you. As you sit with this, you will begin to realize that everything is you. See yourself in everyone and everything.

This is how you transmute violence into kindness.

Tenet 6: Resentment to Forgiveness

Make all actions and deeds reflect the victory of compassion over the ill-tempered outer self.

The discordant EMI holds itself and therefore everyone else in contempt. Anything and anyone, including ourselves, that does not conform and confine to its set of programmed limitations breeds resentment and condemnation. We experience deep inner resentment in the form of self-talk.

Anyone or anything that operates outside of our self-imposed limitations is resented for not obeying and suffering. Misery does love company as like attracts like. Resentment and condemnation are the preferred currencies of exchange between our subconscious patterned egoic minds.

By forgiving and congratulating yourself for not achieving total subservience to your conditioned mind, you will cease to hold resentment toward yourself or anyone else. As you release yourself from misery, all your previous resentment of others will be transmuted into forgiveness. Every notion you give birth to will reflect the inner beauty and geometry of authentic compassion.

MEDITATION
Turn Resentment into Forgiveness

Close your eyes, take a deep breath in through the nose, and exhale out the mouth. Repeat this three times.

Ask yourself, "who is it that holds resentment?" You answer will be, "Me. I'm the one who holds resentment." Now ask yourself, "who am I?"

Your resentment is an illusion just as your human character is. Resentment is the temporary experience of a lack of self-alignment projected outward. Now that you are experiencing the absence of the one who holds resentment, let that space be filled with gratitude for this discovery. Extend that gratitude in the form of forgiveness to everyone and everything your character ever held in resentment.

This is how to move from resentment to forgiveness.

Tenet 7: Weakness to Strength

Anchor your mind and body in tangible truth and all obstacles, sickness, and disease shall be defeated.

The soul (sentience given energy) is the cure for all that ails humanity. It is the only eternal and immutable truth. The love and wisdom that created us (when harnessed properly) dismantles and destroys everything other than itself. Complete alignment to that truth allows one to develop an unshakable mind and indomitable will. The further downstream you are from your own love, the weaker you become in mind, body, and spirit.

The finite mind and physical body are part of and attuned to the local low-frequency environment. Without your complete Higher Mind dominion and mastery over the mind/body complex, both will be greatly and easily affected by everything here. If your mind is weak, the body and will must emulate a similar pathetic nature.

Without mind/body being in rooted and attuned to the Self, your human character will personify weakness and succumb to earthly pressures. Strength is unification with Self. With unbreakable mind/body/spirit alignment to your own Higher Self and Higher Mind, nothing can cast its shadow over the light. Sickness and disease will be cast out. Weakness will not and cannot enter the temple of God.

MEDITATION
Move from Weakness to Strength

Close your eyes, take a deep breath in through the nose, and exhale out the mouth. Repeat this three times.

Place the tips of your middle and index fingers to the center of your chest. Bring all your awareness and attention to the sensation of touch in the center of your chest. Gently, from inside your chest, reach out and touch your fingertips. This fully opens your heart chakra and fully activates your sentience.

Imagine that your human vehicle and its subsequent EMI are simply avatars controlled and created by the immortal sentience in the center of your chest. Imagine that everything that bothers, frightens, or holds back your human character is all part of a video game and not real. Only the sentience that directs, controls, creates, and is forever untouched by everything is real. Imagine what it feels like knowing that what you are (the sentience) can never be defeated, harmed, or destroyed, ever. Imagine what it feels like to be that powerful and immortal. Now, remove your avatar and play the game directly with nothing in the way of your unbreakable strength and ability to create without limitation.

This is how to move from weakness to strength.

Journal what this feels like to have your avatar removed.

Tenet 8: Greed to Generosity

Give and share freely, without fear, and all limitations shall cease to exist.

Greed is a side effect native to the low frequencies of the physical universe. It is birthed by the belief-based parasitical EMI. Its lineage can be traced back to the concept of lack which has been used to promote fear deemed socially acceptable and ultimately deified through the co-opting and weaponization of competition. It is a heavily relied upon directive within the divide-and-conquer sociopathic playbook.

Because the lower conscious collapses and compartmentalizes what is eternally whole, separation is experienced internally and externally. This temporary separation from Self promotes fear and the concept of lack within the finite mind. What ensues is a ferocious and psychopathic tendency to take, accumulate, and hoard at the expense of so-called "others."

Only by tangibly experiencing the eternal completeness of the Self can the parasitical low-frequency programmed EMI be defeated. Simply put, if you don't have it right now, then you don't need it. Whatever notion you give birth to, the multiverse acts as a multi-frequential mirror and energetic multiplier. Generosity begets abundance. The collective tangible understanding of the universal and omnipresent complete One Self within us all will forever transmute greed into generosity.

MEDITATION
Turn Greed into Generosity

Close your eyes, take a deep breath in through the nose, and exhale out the mouth. Repeat this three times.

Pretend your two eyes are not connected to your brain. Imagine that whatever you share freely with others always comes back to you as you need it. Imagine that everything is energy and as you let energy flow through you, you automatically become a larger and larger open conduit of energy, both giving and receiving.

Imagine what this feels like. Imagine what it feels like to be a boundless open conduit for love, joy, and abundance.

Understand that the only block from this exalted state of permanent higher consciousness is your own electromagnetic interference.

This is how to turn greed into generosity.

Journal what it feels like to be a boundless open conduit to give and receive without limitation.

Tenet 9: Limitation to Limitlessness

Align your every desire to the freeing of your mind and body, and the kingdom of heaven shall reign once again.

Desire is the first order of creation. It is also the single most powerful force (from a frequential perspective) we can directly harness to create consciously. To infuse this realm with true divinity—our unconditional love, timeless wisdom, and indomitable will—we must command, with a single point of focus, the freeing of the mind/body complex from all delusions created through misperceptions, misunderstandings, and misidentifications.

The physical realm is as real and limiting in direct correlation with your belief in the authenticity that you are the mind/body complex. The inverse of that statement is also true. Tangibly knowing that you are a supremely higher-dimensional energy being having a temporary human experience allows you to experience yourself as the divine fractal of God that you are.

The kingdom of heaven is here now: it's you. Your Higher Mind, loving heart, and unbreakable spirit is the kingdom of heaven embodied here and now within physical reality. Only your own ignorance and fear prevents the truth and only your transcendence of them can liberate you.

MEDITATION
Move from Limitation to Limitlessness

Close your eyes, take a deep breath in through the nose, and exhale out the mouth. Repeat this three times.

Pretend you just arrived here, no past, no future. Sit down, feet planted firmly on the ground, your back straight with your head tilted slightly downward. Close your eyes. Relax your tongue in the back of your mouth like a clam resting in its shell. Place your hands, palms up, on the upper most part of your thighs. Breathe in deeply from your diaphragm and exhale out your nose. Repeat this breathing three times.

Now, with the utmost fervent desire of your soul, repeat the command, "the body is nothing. The body is nothing. The body is nothing." Do not stop until this eternal truth is tangibly realized and experientially known.

This is how to move from limitation to limitlessness.

Tenet 10: Complexity to Simplicity

Allow "what is" and simply work within the crystalline clarity of now.

Complexity arises the moment we let fear create the thinking mind. By rejecting the clarity of now, endless simulations of past and future disempower you. Non-stop mental machinations and pointless emotionalizations result in delusion of mind and weakness of will. The thinking mind is the chaos and complexity born of fear. Nestled within the simplicity of now, choiceless detachment throws open the door to your Higher Mind and the tangible recognition of your Immortal Self.

Without the chaos and complexity brought upon by the fear-based reactionary EMI, your own towering and eternal presence would be known. The complexity of doubts and ever-present fears overwhelm the underpinnings of trust and faith inherent within the Self. When firmly anchored within the now, mental complexity born of fear is defeated by the simplicity of truth and presence.

By allowing what is to flow, the non-stop complexity and turmoil inherent in trying to make existence fit the paradigm of your limitation program, simplicity and clarity will be tangibly known. Mental and emotional projections will cease and with it, complexity will turn to simplicity.

MEDITATION
Turn Complexity into Simplicity

Close your eyes, take a deep breath in through the nose, and exhale out the mouth. Repeat this three times.

Ask yourself, "Who is it that complicates things?" Your answer will be, "Me. I'm the one who complicates things." Then ask yourself, "Who am I?" You will get no answer because your EMI is simply electromagnetic interference and not you.

Now that your mind is clear and your emotions have stabilized, in the exact same way you give yourself permission to relax physically when you sit or lie down, give yourself permission to fully relax mentally and emotionally. Give yourself complete inner stillness, peace, and silence. Fall in love with the exquisite feeling of simplicity that comes with total mental clarity and emotional balance. Make this simplicity, this feeling, the greatest love of your life.

This is how to turn complexity into simplicity.

Tenet 11: Anger to Compassion

Operate with non-judgment, and loving communion with all life will be tangibly known.

Anger gives us the tangible depth of EMI identifications that have not been satiated. Anger is always in direct proportion to the energetic strength of attachment and hierarchy of importance we have assigned. The more important we have made something, the bigger the energetic attachment is, the greater the anger we experience.

Anger serves an important role in human development. It allows us to tangibly feel our own level of unrealized expectations. It gives us the exact level of non-presence and non-self-awareness we experience in the moment. Anger is one of the most potent learning tools we possess because it portends the possibility of greatest harm to ourselves and others, even when misused as motivation.

Being fully present is compassion. All of you here now. All your love, forgiveness, and divinity emanate from you when you are fully here. From presence compassion flows. Compassion overwhelms, diffuses, and transmutes anger like wisdom embraces, nourishes, and elevates all it encounters.

MEDITATION
Transmute Anger into Compassion

Close your eyes, take a deep breath in through the nose, and exhale out the mouth. Repeat this three times.

Pretend you just arrived here, no past, no future. Imagine that what has made you angry was simply a scene in a movie that you watched. The movie has absolutely nothing to do with you. You just watched it, that's it. It was for entertainment purposes only.

Imagine what it feels like to have watched a movie that you enjoyed and learned something from. Now imagine what it feels like to share that joy and useful information with someone, and it helps them. Imagine what it feels like to have what was once your pain but has turned into joy and wisdom help heal and save someone.

This is how to transmute anger into compassion.

Tenet 12: Desire to Stillness

Practice non-engagement with the egoic mind and non-identification with the physical body, and true divinity will reveal itself.

It is the amount of attention and authenticity in your identifications to the programmed desires of finite mind and sensations of physical body that give it such power. Underneath it all resides eternal divinity, timeless perfection, and unbreakable stillness.

Desire born of personhood only increases the disharmonious experience and weight of personhood. The more you desire and strive at the behest of your EMI, the more real and all-consuming your EMI becomes. Tracing the core motivation that fuels your desires (not acting upon them) is the only way to know your Self.

Only the desire to know God will ever free you from earthly desire. God is within your consciousness not outside of it. Set your desire and intention to know that which created and lives within you, and in everyone else, and all other desires will cease.

MEDITATION
Turn Desire into Stillness

Close your eyes, take a deep breath in through the nose, and exhale out the mouth. Repeat this three times.

Imagine that your mind/body complex is a biological spacesuit. You (sentience given energy) are simply wearing this spacesuit. You have no name, image, or form. Imagine that every thought is just the action of sentience sending energy into the mental body. What results are thoughts based upon identifications you mistakenly made during this trip to Earth.

Now imagine sending no energy anywhere through total and complete rest through gentle concentration. All your energy sits between your belly button and groin. All your sentience sits between your heart and spine. Give yourself permission to just be here now. Nothing but pure presence and unsullied awareness.

Imagine what it feels like to sink so far back into yourself that the mind/body complex requires no effort to engage it. You have no need to engage the biological suit because they run on their own without you. You are inside, protected, perfect, whole, and complete without them.

This is how to turn desire into stillness.

Appendix 2
The 12 Timeless Truths to Raise Your Frequency

Below are the twelve timeless truths of Self-mastery, their respective explanations and specific exercises that accompany each of the teachings.

Timeless Truth 1

We are not the mind/body complex but the eternal Creator Awareness of all experience and non-experience.

What you are exists well before the mind/body was created and will exist well afterward its demise. You (eternal creator awareness) are the I Am. You are the unchanging, unscathed, untouched creator awareness of all experience and non-experience. You are immortal, infinite, and limitless. You are beyond all labels, and have no name, image, or form.

You (I Am) create endlessly for all eternity to learn about your infinite capacity for ever-growing love and timeless wisdom, and thus ultimately know that you are God/Source/Creator as well.

EXERCISE
Accessing Your Expansiveness

Create without judgment. Go to the beach, the forest, the lake, the mountains, the park. Create an experience without allowing the subconscious patterned egoic mind to infiltrate. Experience the creator and unsullied awareness within you directly. Flow as this and do not stop. Become acutely aware of what "you" feel like, your state of being, your vibration, your state of consciousness, your expansiveness, your joy. Then journal this experience without any judgment.

Timeless Truth 2

We are sentience given a body of energy that exists within and beyond space-time concurrently.

You are sentience (divine intelligence) that eternally exists well before humanity was created and you will exist well after all humanity has completed its existence. You (I Am) are unconditional love and timeless wisdom, whose subsets are talents and abilities, that is given energy to create utilizing your imagination: the true mind of God. They—you—sentience and energy—are all aspects of your Higher Self, your Totality. You are an aspect of your Higher Self, and your Higher Self is a fractal of God.

Your Higher Self or Totality exists well beyond space-time while you are an aspect/projection of that and concurrently exist here within space-time. You are the part of your Higher Self that is having a temporary low-frequency human experience. You (I Am) are experiencing the temporary confines of body consciousness within space-time, while concurrently your Higher Self lives and resides well beyond and outside space-time. You are your Higher Self, just less in volume, and it is you. You are here now, and the rest of you (your Higher Self) is outside space-time now, and concurrently.

EXERCISE
Recognize Awareness Within and Beyond Time

Stop thinking. Meditate using any of my techniques. Realize that in full presence—complete being-ness here and now—that you are always aware of your unsullied awareness. That is the concurrent within space-time and outside of it all at once. The little you is the bigger you and vice versa. Fall in love with this knowingness and live this way.

Journal what this realization gives you.

Timeless Truth 3

The ego/mind/identity (EMI) is a limitation program that runs by thinking and not the Self directly.

The ego/mind/identity (EMI) is the human character we create due to incarnation into the lower frequencies of the physical universe. Your personality is your personal reality. Your EMI is a creation, your creation, that is birthed from the Self (I Am) but is not the Self directly. This is why you are aware of *everything* your EMI experiences and creates. Every thought, emotion, action, experience, and behavior you are *aware* of. You are the *awareness* of your physical body and every bodily sensation. That pure awareness (not the judgment/analysis of it) is the Self directly: the I Am.

Just like God, as we are an indirect fractal of God, the Self (I Am) holds no judgment. The I Am is pure imagination born of the eternal wellspring of love and wisdom. It is your EMI, your human character, that imprisons your free consciousness and pure body of energy in a state of self-judgment, non-acceptance, and suffering through thinking. The I Am imagines through love and wisdom. The EMI imprisons itself through thinking, trapping itself in a past and future.

The EMI is always in direct proportion to the love you withhold from yourself. This lack of love is tangibly produced and experienced through thought. Your thoughts are based upon what your EMI is built from and identifies itself with, starting with the physical body.

It further grows based upon what your five senses perceive, such as beliefs, concepts, experiences, ideologies, so-called knowledge, and feelings that you choose to misidentify your I Am with.

EXERCISE
Seeing the I Am

Look in the mirror. Do not judge, label, categorize, or analyze yourself. In that state, discover who is really looking through your eyes when there is no judgment. Journal who/what is doing the seeing. Write about the qualities of the who/what that looks through the eyes on non-judgment. What does this feel like to see your I Am in this way?

Timeless Truth 4

The Self (I Am) is already perfect, whole, and complete,
and remains changeless through happiness, misery, life, and death.

The Self (I Am) is not touched, affected, sullied, or harmed regardless of all experience. That is because I Am is beyond all experience. You (I Am) create experiences to understand, know, and learn about the limitless depth and capability of what you really are. All experience is simply the play of your own imagination, which is ultimately the Higher Mind of Source/God/Creator learning about itself through you.

The I Am (sentience) evolves through the tangible accruing of more and more of what it already and always is—love and wisdom. Through experience your reservoir of unconditional love and timeless wisdom (sentience) deepens. As this occurs your heart softens, and your will strengthens. Concurrently, the energy you are given and learn to commandeer increases. Evolution is the accrual of love and wisdom and along with it, you literally become more and more powerful.

EXERCISE
Finding Unbreakable Security

Imagine the worst natural disaster possible. Imagine it goes on for days, weeks, months, years, decades, even lifetimes. Now look at the sun. Would the worst weather, for eons of time, even touch the sun? You (I Am) is the sun. No matter what happens to mind/body, good or bad, it never actually touches you. Ever. Feel what that ultimate, eternal, and unbreakable security feels like. Let that feeling permeate your entire mind, body, and soul. Stay that way until it's permanent. Journal what this feels like.

Timeless Truth 5

The True Self (I Am) is eternal awareness and can only be directly experienced through the cessation of sensory analysis.

The I Am exists before the mind/body complex. Through incarnation into the lower frequencies of the physical universe, the EMI is created through personhood. That creation (the subconscious patterned egoic mind) is what analyzes and judges.

It is only through detachment supported through meditation does one begin to experience the quieting of the egoic mind and bodily sensations. Inner stillness and silence allow awareness to reside and dwell within its source point—I Am. Normalizing this state is liberation from the tyranny of the ego mind and the only true measure of success.

EXERCISE
No Puppeteer

Imagine that you are a puppet—no brain and no bones—but there is no puppeteer. There is only an unseen force, an energy, moving through you, animating your body, making your heart beat, your lungs breathe, and your eyes see. Journal what this feels like.

Go about your day, knowing there is no brain, just an unseen force carrying you, giving life to you. Journal what it's like to live like this for a day.

Timeless Truth 6

Existence simply exists to know itself and all its infinite potential.

Existence is just beginning to become self-aware. It endlessly creates endless creations to understand itself fully. Because there is no end or beginning to existence itself, there is only limitless imagination and infinite possibilities. Infinite possible possibilities. The infinite possibility of possible possibilities of possible possibilities. You (I Am) are exactly that.

As you create, you learn about yourself. As you create more fully, more consciously, more self-aware, your creations reflect more of what you eternally and directly are at your core—love, wisdom, and power. Your highest good is everyone's highest good simultaneously and concurrently. This is to know God and to create like a Master of One Self. The One Self within us all.

EXERCISE
Leaving Earthly Desires

Just for today, do not seek anything through physical gratification or mental understandings. Meditate long enough that all earthly desires leave you. The whole, complete, eternal Self will be tangibly known. By journaling, discover what it is that the Self (the I Am) actually desires.

Timeless Truth 7

Right and wrong, the past and the future, real or imagined,
life and death are all concepts and are of no
consequence to the Immortal Self.

There is only one moment of creation seen from an infinite number of perspectives. The concept you hold of yourself is merely a single viewpoint within a sea of endless viewpoints. Therefore, it is a singular momentary contraction, a limitation, and only matters to the creator/identifier of the single viewpoint: the temporary human character. Alter your viewpoint, your perception by expanding your inner understanding, and everything changes even though nothing has changed. You change—the I Am creator creates—and everything changes because you are everything.

You can change one thousand times in a single day and still be wearing the same clothes. The Immortal Self (I Am) does not require self-confining parameters like mental concepts or a physical vehicle. Your human character (the EMI) is disconnected from the I Am and therefore clings to illusions instead. This is why and how your human character tangibly experiences the concepts of past and future, real or imagined, life and death, separation and lack.

EXERCISE
Shift into Allowance

Take any past event that you have held, accepted, and agreed to from your current level of understanding, viewpoint, or fixed reality. Perhaps it's your parents not understanding the way you live your life or a break-up you've had with a partner. Now simply expand and shift into allowance. Allow that moment to simply be just one way the infinite possible possibilities can reveal and express themselves to you. This gives you and the event permission to shift out of a fixed reality and into the spaciousness of the Immortal Self and all its infinite viewpoints. Choose three traumatic events in your life. Journal by applying this shift on how those events now feel/are perceived.

Timeless Truth 8

All forms, whether tangible or intangible are manifestation of Source/God/Creator but to know Source/God/Creator directly, one must remain as one began, unsullied by the tangible or intangible.

I Am is the only absolute, ultimate, and eternal truth. With each notion we give birth not born directly from the purity, majesty, and clarity of I Am; We ease God out. I Am is Source/God/Creator. Any identification we make after "I Am" is untrue, and thus we take ourselves further and further away from the source point of ourselves. We then tangibly suffer our own misperception, misunderstanding, and misidentification.

"I Am (add anything)" is the act of creation itself. The painter is not the painting. Remain unsullied and only be, act, behave, speak as I Am. That state is the direct gateway to Source/God/Creator. There is no experience of the EMI or disharmony as I Am. There can be no discord in non-thought and non-identification. I Am is the door to total clarity, eternal calmness, heightened connectivity, full communion, and unbreakable courage.

EXERCISE
Experiencing Non-thought

Stand in front of a mirror. Use the instantaneous meditation technique of pretending your two physical eyes are not connected to your brain. Experience non-thought. Now repeat the mantra "I am the conqueror of my mind and body" until this is tangibly experienced and there is no turning back. Journal what you feel like once this is accomplished.

Timeless Truth 9

All limitations are self-imposed.

Existence is all one. There are no blocks or limitations in "what is." We create blocks of limitation namely through identification with maya such as beliefs, concepts, ideologies, or so-called knowledge. This occurs due to self-imposed body consciousness (EMI). There is no resistance to anything. Existence is all one. We create resistance and therefore the experience of limitation through identification. We do this incessantly by thinking and emoting.

You are your Higher Mind. You are your Higher Self, just less in total volume. We are a bubble of pure sentient imagination within the Higher Mind of Source/God/Creator. Freedom from the tyranny of the subconscious patterned egoic mind gives you the tangible experience of your true and eternal limitless nature.

Limitations are created by our identification with creations. Creations are not the creator directly. By identifying with any creation, we create our own self-imposed limitation. We are such powerful creators, but we are creating from the subconscious patterned egoic mind. We have yet to consciously create directly from our own perfection and divinity but rather from the self-imposed limitations of the low-frequency logic/linearity paradigm of the reactionary thinking mind.

EXERCISE
Exploring Limitations

What is your highest desire? Write it down. Now write down what holds you back from achieving this and how that feels. Then write down something from your mundane daily to-do list. Now write down what holds you back from achieving this and how that feels.

Deeply examine the feeling/energetic quality between the block you assign to achieving your highest desire and the feeling/energetic block you assign from a mundane chore. Realize the feeling/energetic quality that you assign is, in actuality, the only difference between these two things being achieved. The energetic feeling, weight, meaning, gravitas you assign to the block is the only difference. All limitations are self-imposed.

Timeless Truth 10

We are always waking up to the infinite possible possibilities contained within every single now *while housed within a multi-frequential and multi-dimensional structure.*

Which *now* we experience and inwardly shift to is based upon personal and collective creativity in regards to what we most fervently desire to experience, moment to moment, based upon our level of sentient self-awareness and vibration.

Within every single *now* is the complete, full, and in-depth totality of infinite possibilities. We (sentience) endlessly shift our inner perception and self-understanding. This inner expansion/contraction results in the changes we tangibly experience in the so-called outer world.

Because each soul is unique, we are seeing and experiencing the infinite variety of choices one can make within every single now. As humanity is guided and taught from timeless wisdom and unconditional love, it will begin to tangibly experience these greater aspects and qualities within themselves. This will result in a higher-frequency perspective and choices available. This will subsequently be reflected in the changes we shall see in the so-called outer world.

EXERCISE
Actor or Actions

Look at a situation you feel stuck in and powerless to change. Shift from the state of acceptance and agreement that this is the one and only reality into the state of allowance of the infinite possible possibilities to reveal themselves within the screen of your consciousness.

Journal what the tangible difference is between acceptance and allowance. Stay in this expanded state of allowance and see what happens to your state of being in regard to everything that you previously accepted and agreed to that was discordant to you.

Timeless Truth 11

We move—not time—by the choices we make,
and this "movement" is either the evolution
or regression of consciousness.

What we experience as physical movement is, in actuality, a shift in perception. The I Am is endlessly experiencing the infinite facets of itself. It is either expanding its self-awareness or contracting its tangible understanding of itself. What we call movement is simply the shadow of illusion our light casts as it shifts in inner perception.

In the no-mind pure state of consciousness, there is no tangible recognition of the actor performing actions or physical movement. That is because both the actor and its actions are an illusion. They are simply a play within the outer screen of your consciousness. This outer play of actor and movement is always directed at the behest of the I Am-ness.

The I Am—while exploring its own limitless depth—projects a so-called person who perform actions to see itself in the act of experiencing, learning, and evolving itself. In the one true reality that eternally exists well beyond the five physical senses and the intellect, there is no outer world, no person, no actions, no movement. Simply, I Am.

EXERCISE
Revealing Infinite Possible Possibilities

Look at every action your actor has ever performed. Are you that human actor and its actions, or are you the awareness of that actor and its actions? If you are neither actor nor actions, how do they arise within your consciousness? What is actually—tangibly—occurring?

Has either actor or actions ever touched the I Am? Look deeply at this and journal your new understanding of actor/movement/actions.

Timeless Truth 12

*Source/God/Creator is the summation of all wisdom—
unconditional love—and expresses itself by endowing humanity
with the free will to experience whatever it most desires,
always on its return journey from nowhere to where we eternally
remain: the Oneness of unconditional love.*

We ultimately go nowhere as we eternally remain inside and part of Source/God/Creator. There is only here and now. Consciousness simply creates challenges and obstacles so it can see itself in the act of overcoming them. This is the only real evolution: the accrual of sentience. You and your life plan are just that. It is a microcosm of the macrocosm.

Your Higher Self creates you so it can evolve through and as you. Your Higher Self was created by Source/God/Creator so it can evolve and learn about itself concurrently. Its core, the very wellspring of being and non-being, is the vibration of love. The further we get away from the essence of ourselves, the further we get away from the only truth: love.

The only death and discord we ever experience is the love we withhold from ourselves, and therefore each other. Give yourself what you most fervently desire: your own love. Surrender and let your heart explode *now* and it shall dissolve all that cannot endure such perfection, majesty, and divinity. God is waiting, patiently, and only yearns for your love.

EXERCISE
Pure Love

What does love actually feel like? What are its tangible qualities? Journal and explore this. Love precedes all mental concepts and bodily sensations. Search your heart deeply. Open your heart and make your mind realize its Master. Just for today, only act in complete accordance with this love. With every notion you give birth to let it be an act of pure love. Let it envelop your entire being. Journal this and never betray yourself, your love, again.

Final Message

The world that we know is possible is our destiny. All of us are creating an empire built upon unconditional love and timeless wisdom. The enlightened teachings contained within this book along with my first two books (*Supercharged Self-Healing* and *Change Your Mind)* are foundation of the new earth. This new earth, the new age we are creating right now, will need new teachers. That is you, my friend. You.

We made this promise to each other eons ago. To usher in The Wisdom That Transcends Knowledge. It is happening as you read this. My will cannot be broken, not even by death, and neither can yours now that it's aligned and awakened to the truth.

You have all my attention and love, now and forever.

Join me in liberation, freedom, and Self-mastery. I have been waiting for you... Welcome home.

I am your holy brother,

RJ

To Write to the Author

If you wish to contact the author or would like more information about this book, please write to the author in care of Llewellyn Worldwide Ltd. and we will forward your request. Both the author and the publisher appreciate hearing from you and learning of your enjoyment of this book and how it has helped you. Llewellyn Worldwide Ltd. cannot guarantee that every letter written to the author can be answered, but all will be forwarded. Please write to:

RJ Spina
℅ Llewellyn Worldwide
2143 Wooddale Drive
Woodbury, MN 55125-2989

Please enclose a Self-addressed stamped envelope for reply, or $1.00 to cover costs. If outside the U.S.A., enclose an international postal reply coupon.

Many of Llewellyn's authors have websites with additional information and resources. For more information, please visit our website at http://www.llewellyn.com.

Notes

Notes

Notes

Notes

Notes